ignite 1
THE DYNAMITE

Ignite the Dynamite

© Daniel Hagen 2022

First published 2022

Published by Daniel Hagen Ministries

www.danielhagenministries.com

All rights reserved. Without limiting the rights under copyright reserved above, no part of this publication may be reproduced, stored in or introduced into a database and retrieval system or transmitted in any form or any means (electronic, mechanical, photocopying, recording or otherwise) without the prior written permission of both the owner of copyright and the above publishers. The only exception is brief quotations in printed reviews.

Printed by IngramSpark

ISBN 9780645472202

ISBN Ebook: 9780645472219

Unless otherwise specified, all scripture taken from the New King James Version®. Copyright © 1982 by Thomas Nelson. Used by permission. All rights reserved.

Cover design by Katherine Munro

Ignite The Dynamite

Acknowledgements	4
Foreword - Ben Fitzgerald	6
Endorsements	9
Daniel's Journey	14
The Empowerment Of The Holy Spirit	27
Demons And Deliverance	41
Discipled in Healing	63
It's For All Believers	79
Cessationism	87
Character Before Anointing	106
Signs And Wonders with the Truth	120
Raising the Dead	133
Frank's Journey	147
Dunamis Power By Frank Clancy	154
Dreams And Visions	163
The Power of the Gospel	181
References	197

ACKNOWLEDGEMENTS

I would like to thank Chris and Jess Hockridge. Your help on this project was massive. Thank you so much for your tireless and selfless efforts in research and the putting together of the manuscript. I seriously could not have completed this without you both.

Also, a big thanks to Anton and Bev Bekker. Your role in helping review and edit this book has been invaluable.

Kathrine Munro, thank you so much for your anointed art work.

Brett Shaw, thank you for the editing and production of the audiobook.

Frank Clancy, as I stated in this book, you have been such an inspiration and mentor in my life. It was such an honour having you contribute two chapters. I know the people reading this book will be blown away and inspired by your life and teaching, just as I am. Thanks to both you and Denny for your on-going prayer and support!

Ben Fitzgerald thank you for being such an ongoing source of encouragement and inspiration. Having you write the foreword was such a blessing.

Mum and Dad (Tony & Irene Hagen), love you so much. Thank you for helping me piece together my journey to ensure it's accuracy, and I especially thank you for your continuous love, prayer and support.

Finally, last but certainly not least, thanks to my wife Chelsea and my four beautiful children; Reece, Esther, Caleb and Abby. Apart from Jesus you guys are my greatest inspiration. Thank you for doing life and running this race with me. All for Jesus!

FOREWORD - BEN FITZGERALD

I am so honoured to have been asked to write the foreword for such an amazing man, friend, and author. Daniel is living a life reflective of what he has penned here. Not only does he have strong theology, but he has also worked out the truth of scripture through obedience in his own life.

In the seventeen years that I've known Daniel Hagen, I can barely remember a moment where he wasn't convicted with a deep longing to love God more. He has always had a profound sense of hunger for Heaven's power to be displayed on the Earth. That conviction has led him on a daily basis into the lives of countless people who didn't yet know Jesus. It has also led him to equip and challenge the family of God. In this book, Daniel challenges every believer to live in the fullness of the Holy Spirit's outpouring, that the Prophets foretold.

Daniel dives into one of the primary reasons the Spirit of God was given to us. He unpacks the dynamite power of God to equip us as witnesses on the Earth and to walk in the power of God to fulfil that mission.

I don't know about you, but I get a lot more confident when

I know the reason and have surety as to why I am doing something. Daniel's book brilliantly infuses you with confidence as he unpacks the pure Word of God and gives much-needed language and understanding. Ignite the Dynamite is full of phenomenal testimonies and examples of everyday people who have seen God transform lives. It's not only for the ministers, this book unpacks how the everyday believer can deliver others of demons, heal the sick, and even see the salvation of thousands of people.

These practical examples and stories whet your appetite for more of Him and become keys on how to activate your faith to ignite the dynamite power of God in your life. No matter what denomination you come from, or what your understanding of the person of the Holy Spirit has been; it's clear that we can all agree if Jesus was filled with the Spirit and needed the "dunamis" power of God, then how much more do we need to personally understand His presence in our lives!

I will finish with this statement of how I felt as I read the book and why it impacted me so much. The reason I cannot recommend Ignite the Dynamite enough, and why I encourage you to be hungry as you read it, is because on each page all I could sense is purity. The purity of Scripture, and the purity of the Holy Spirit. The purity of the man writing the book, and the purity of how God wants to equip you and change you as you read it. His plans for you are greater than we could ever fathom. So get ready and open your heart for Him to ignite His ways in you as you learn from Him. I cannot wait to hear the stories of the lives and nations that were changed by those who read this.

Ben Fitzgerald.
Senior leader - Awakening Europe

ENDORSEMENTS

Bill Johnson

Ignite the Dynamite by Daniel Hagen

From experiencing drug-induced mania to becoming a powerful minister of the gospel, Daniel Hagen's life reveals the freedom and power available to all who give their life to Christ. Our God is in the business of total transformation, and Ignite the Dynamite highlights testimony after testimony of God's life-changing love. Let this book stir your heart for what the normal Christian life looks like— one filled with purity, passion, and power.

Bill Johnson
Author of Open Heavens and Born for Significance
Bethel Church, Redding, CA

Tim Hall

Daniel Hagen is a unique man of God. His massive size and long dreadlocks make him appear unlike any minister you are likely to meet. He does not fit the world's perceived idea of a Christian minister but appears more like an ancient prophet who walks out of a desert place with fire in his eyes and an explosion of power in his words. Indeed this is Daniel! He is a firebrand in the hand of God. He is fearless, bold, powerfully anointed and driven with a passion to see multitudes swept into the Kingdom of God. He is a man who truly believes that the Kingdom of God is not just in word but raw power. He lives what he preaches alongside his anointed wife Chelsea and their wonderful children.

This book will inspire and challenge you to a supernatural and powerfully effective life with God. Daniel's ongoing story has inspired me personally in a very real way. His daring faith and passion to live a totally Spirit driven life will be imparted to you in every page of this great book.

Tim Hall
Leading Australian Evangelist
Tim Hall International Ministries

Margaret Court

This book is a must read!

In this book, Daniel shares his testimony of where he's come from and how Jesus has saved him from a life of darkness. His story will help many people come out of the enemy's kingdom and into the light, displaying that we can walk in victory through our Lord Jesus Christ!

Daniel challenges you to walk in intimacy with God and to be bold and courageous in reaching the unsaved. It is about the simplicity of being a vessel of honour for Christ, not formulas, but being a doer of God's Word.

This book is a 'NOW' book for our Nation.

Thank you Daniel for being honest and sharing your heart and encouraging the Body of Christ to step out in grace and faith to take the love of Jesus Christ to a lost and dying world.

Rev Margaret Court AC, MBE
Senior Pastor - Victory Life Centre Inc. Perth Western Australia
President, Victory Life International Bible Training Centre Inc.
President, VLCS Inc. (T/A Margaret Court Community Outreach)

Shaun Marler

Every now and then, a book is written that is a word in season from the heart of God for the hour we are living in. This book is one such book! I encourage all Believers to get a copy of this book and read it! Whether you have been a Christian for one week or twenty years, this book will bless and inspire you to reach, move in and demonstrate the miracle power of God. Pastor Daniel unpacks the scriptures, making them food and inspiration for your life to flow in the same power that Jesus Christ and the Apostles operated in. Pastor Daniel clearly demonstrates that this power is available to us all today. Not only is it available, but if we are going to see our world won for Christ, it is absolutely essential that we, the Believers, walk in, live in and operate this power!

Over the time that I have known Pastor Daniel, I can testify that what you are about to read is not just teaching but how Daniel lives his life! He lives and breathes what he teaches! He has personally been a blessing to my family and my own life! You will love the testimonies, the examples and the faithbuilding words! You will be refreshed, inspired and encouraged to push in, go for and receive God's best! By applying this teaching and principles to your life, you will see miracles, and you will win souls for Jesus!

Dr. Shaun Marler
Published Author, Teacher and Senior Pastor World Harvest Ministries, QLD, Australia

DANIEL'S JOURNEY

My Journey To Christ

My journey with Jesus begins with my parents.

When I was just a young boy, my Mum and Dad were a young married couple who were struggling in their marriage. For months they were seeking whether God was real and they were questioning the purpose of their lives.

At this time, my Dad was a farmer who would tend to the fields early in the mornings. One night, when he was 25 years old, my Dad went into the field and experienced something that would shift his entire family's lives — he had a radical encounter with Jesus!

Dad recalls that he was driving his tractor in the pitch-blackness of the night at 3am. Suddenly, everything around him lit up! Dad says it was as though time became still and all that he could see was light. We now know that Dad was experiencing an open vision! In this vision Jesus appeared to him and said audibly, "Tony, I've called you to be my soldier."

It is so phenomenal that in the months leading up to this encounter my Mum and Dad were seeking truth in their own way.

It really is true when the Bible says if you seek Him with all your heart you shall find Him! (Jeremiah 29:13).

My Dad was shocked and rocked to his core by this awesome encounter with Jesus. Dad had a Catholic upbringing, so he had a little experience with religion, but this was his first real encounter with the living God, Jesus Christ! And after coming face-to-face with Jesus, the first thing Dad did after he finished work was rush home to share with Mum what had happened.

Growing up, Mum had limited experience with religion. She recalls attending religious education in school and being open and drawn to what the Teacher was sharing at the time. Mum even recited the sinner's prayer when she was 15 years old after someone had dropped a gospel tract in her letterbox. She was greatly impacted that day, but she didn't tell anybody until years later. There was something deep within Mum's heart that wanted to connect with God, but she just didn't know how to act on it.

Fast forward six years, she's married to my Dad and he comes home from his shift in the fields bursting with excitement. My Dad tells my Mum that he's just had a crazy encounter with Jesus! This is same miracle-working Jesus who drew her heart through a gospel tract six years earlier! Mum was very open to hear what he had to say!

Dad eagerly told her the entire story. And as he was sharing about his open vision of Jesus, there came a knock at the door.

Normally my Dad wouldn't open the door to strangers. In fact, usually he would tell random door-knockers, especially people holding Bibles, where they could go! But on this already strange day, my Dad decided to open the door and it was a Christian Pastor! The Pastor tells Dad that he's in the area door-knocking to ask if anyone was interested in doing a Bible study. Mum and Dad immediately invited the Pastor in and they began to study the Word of God! And from that day onwards, the Pastor came to our house once a week for Bible study with Mum and Dad.

As a small child I remember being plugged into the Church. I have memories of the prayer meetings and of Mum and Dad leading worship for the music teams. It was fun times!

For a long time, Mum and Dad enjoyed attending and serving their home Church in a town called Cranbourne in Australia. Also around this time they began visiting the night service of the main campus in a nearby town called Dandenong. The Church was planted by an amazing minister named Tim Hall, and his meetings were wild! Dynamite power was released in those meetings; the sick were healed, devils were cast out, miracles flowed, and Mum and Dad were baptised in the Holy Spirit! There was a strong emphasis on evangelism and people would come straight from the streets into the meetings and be saved! In fact, my aunties and uncles also began to be saved and baptised in the Holy Spirit at these revival meetings. It truly was an impactful time in the lives of my family! Even as a kid I would go with Mum and Dad and attend all night prayer meetings and experience the power of the Holy Spirit.

However, no Church is perfect, and sometimes people make terrible mistakes. Sadly, my Mum and Dad became hurt by some serious things that were taking place in their home Church in Cranbourne. Mum and Dad were 7 years into their journey and I was around the age of 10. The Church split and
Mum and Dad became somewhat disillusioned and discouraged. As a family we began to search for a new Church, but nothing felt like the right fit. At that time Tim Hall had moved on from Dandenong and they struggled to find a new place to call home. Or perhaps Mum and Dad struggled to reconcile the hurt that they were feeling. Either way, the weeks went by, then months went by and then the years went by and we no longer attended Church.

Slowly, the enemy began to really attack our family and we fell into a place of deception. This is what my family would describe as a wilderness season. They had turned their back on the Church, but thankfully, they didn't turn their back fully on Jesus. Mum and Dad recall that they would still pray to Jesus from time to time, but as a family we were no longer in fellowship, no longer in Christian influence, and no longer reading and studying the Bible.

As a kid entering my pre-teens and then teen years, not having any Christian influence was pretty devastating. I began to go down a pretty dark track. Especially once I formed a band around the age of 16. It wasn't long before my band took off, and by the time I was 18 we were playing in all the popular nightclubs of our city. We even had various record labels trying to sign us. It's weird, but I had actually fallen in love with music at Church. As a boy I watched Mum and Dad be part of the worship teams and that's where I really began to love music. Like my Mum and Dad, God also gave me a gift for music, but as a teenager I began to use that gift for twisted purposes and I became what I describe now as 'the devil's worship leader'. I influenced people in dark things; drugs, alcohol, and other wickedness. It was pretty devastating for my family. I quickly spiralled out of control and became addicted to speed, cocaine, ecstasy, marijuana — In fact, I was addicted to whatever I could put in my body.

Around this time in my life was my introduction to the dark and demonic side of things. I know now that drugs are not a new hook or strategy of the devil. In fact, pagans have been using drugs to tap into the spiritual realm for many years. The Book of Revelation in the Bible uses an English word called 'sorcery'. The original Greek word used in the Bible for 'sorcery' is 'pharmakeia',[1] and it's also where we get our word 'drugs' from. So, drugs and witchcraft are actually closely associated. Mind-altering drugs are a way that people can tap into the spirit realm, whether knowingly or unknowingly. These types of drugs open doors and give access to demonic spirits in people's lives, and that's what happened to me. We will unpack this further in our chapter *Demons & Deliverance*.

As I went deeper into the kingdom of darkness I became more and more demon *oppressed* until finally I was completely given over to it and had become demon *possessed*. The Doctors and the people around me described what was happening to me as paranoid schizophrenia and bipolar. I was having dark, demonic experiences. At one point I thought I was communicating with dead relatives, when really, they were familiar, demonic spirits.

Things got so out of control that even my drug dealer was freaked out. I personally don't have a lot of clear memories from that time period. However, Mum and Dad recall this one time I had overdosed and my dealer called my parents saying, "Come pick him up, I don't want him to die here".

I was totally out of control and there was only one thing that could cure me. It wasn't psychologists. It wasn't psych-wards. There were no 'self-help' measures that could have saved me— and Mum and Dad knew that. They realised that only the miracle-working, dynamite power of God could save me. So, they began to pray, pray, pray! And you know what; their prayers began to work! There is nothing more powerful than praying parents! I am so incredibly grateful for their persistence in spiritual warfare over my soul. Without Mum and Dad contending in prayer, I truly believe I would be in hell.

I remember around this time I had been on a 3-day drug binge. It's funny, but back then there's a lot of hazy memories because I used to be out of it from drugs and lack of sleep. But I remember this as though it was yesterday; I had been up for 3-days and I remember standing in the front yard of our house. I looked over to see my neighbours with their two kids coming out to the letterbox. They were so excited and happy together. There was something so pure about watching this family become so excited about collecting their mail. And in the midst of my drug induced chaos, I had a moment of clarity. A clear thought pierced my mind where I asked myself, "How did I get so messed up?"

God then brought to my memory what life had been like when I was a little kid going to the prayer meetings. Suddenly I heard what felt like an internal voice that shook me to my core. God clearly spoke to me saying, "If you're ever going to get out of this, you need to go back to Church".

Now, at this point I wasn't aware that my Mum and Dad were fervently praying for me. They had phoned a local Pastor and other family members to help them pray around the house I was living in. They would declare truth and tear down strongholds in the spirit realm! They took their authority in Christ and waged prayerful warfare against the enemy for my soul! I believe it was in that moment of clarity, when I heard the voice of the Lord, that their prayers were answered. That voice rocked me so much that, not long after, I decided to walk to a local Church!

As I mentioned, I didn't know my parents had phoned a Pastor to pray with them for my salvation. But guess what— I walked into a Church and the Pastor was Frank Clancy, the very same Pastor who came alongside my parents to pray for my salvation!

The very same Pastor who, to this day, is my mentor and is even a contributor to this book!

It was in Pastor Frank's Church that I was first rocked by the power of the Holy Spirit and was delivered from demons and drug addiction. That day I encountered the miracle-working dynamite power of God! All my chains broke and I was filled with a joy and innocence that I had never known before. The year was 2003, and I have never been the same since! From that moment onwards, I was in love with Jesus and His Church. I knew my destiny and purpose was to serve Jesus and His Church and help others encounter the same power that had set me free.

My life was reborn in the dynamite power of God. I believe that is one of the reasons why I am so passionate about this topic today. Nothing else can truly set someone free! It is only the power of Christ. I think it's quite fitting that my first book is on the miracle working power of God. If it wasn't for the dynamite power of God, I would be dead and in hell!

As I previously stated, I am so grateful to my praying parents! There really is nothing more powerful than praying parents! I also want to thank them for training me up in the ways of God. My life is a testimony to the promise in Proverbs 22:6, *"Train up a child in the way he should go, And when he is old he will not depart from it"*.

I am so grateful to Jesus. I am so grateful that He is the same yesterday, today and forever. He's still setting the captives free, still breaking chains, still casting out devils. His power is still active to see the sick healed!

That is my journey on how I came to know the One who translates us out of the kingdom of darkness and into the Kingdom of His marvellous light. Amen.

Life Since Salvation

Once I was saved in 2003, I continued to radically surrender my life to Jesus Christ. God was redeeming my life that was messed up from drugs and demons. It was around this time of having encountered God, that our band became very successful and was on the verge of scoring a six-figure record deal! However, once I was born-again, I began to write songs that expressed my affection toward God. This really bothered the owner of our management group. So, one day, he called for a meeting, sat us down, and told us, "This industry is full of drug dealers and pimps. Stop talking about Jesus and stop singing about God if you want any more funds invested in the band".

But it was too late; I was too in love with Jesus and there was no way in hell I was going back to a life of brokenness and compromise! Immediately, I walked away from the lure of a life of fame and fortune. I had found my new passion; knowing the Father and making Him known to the nations. I quickly recognised the urgent need to share the life-giving message of Christ to anyone who would listen. Pursuing the heart of God far outweighed any riches the world could offer me. The Bible says, *"For what will it profit a man if he gains the whole world, and loses his own soul?"* (Mark 8:35).

Through my local Church, I started leading teams of everyday believers out onto the streets to preach the gospel. We would openly declare the life-giving message of Christ and demonstrate His love through the miracle-working dynamite power of God! I was once the devil's worship leader, but now I was leading the charge to take back souls for the Kingdom of God.

In 2008, God gave me a beautiful wife, Chelsea, who is deeply in love with Jesus! And together we were released to go and plant Churches. Chelsea and I have spent our lives together planting Churches in Australia with our now four beautiful children.

As well as planting and overseeing Churches in Australia, I have also had the wonderful opportunity to preach Jesus and ignite the dynamite in over thirty nations around the world. I've seen thousands and thousands of people saved, healed and delivered! I'm still blown away at how God can take a messed-up life and turn it into something beautiful!

In 2014, I teamed up with my best-friend, Ben Fitzgerald, and helped him launch Awakening Music. I once used my gift as a musician for the enemy, but now I was using my gift for the glory of God! I was leading worship in some of the greatest evangelistic gatherings of our modern times. I remember as a teenager when I first started getting into the band-life, I would dream of playing in large arenas and stadiums around the world. But when I got saved, I was willing to lay that all down because my heart was to only pursue the will of God. It's funny how years later I've had the opportunity to fulfil that teenage dream. Only this time it's not for an empty and fickle selfish purpose: it's for the glory of God and seeing thousands of people receive Jesus Christ as their Lord and Saviour!

In the following chapters, I have purposely chosen to share most of my miracle stories from early on in my Christian walk. My heart is that I want every reader to be inspired and equipped to operate in the dynamite power of God. The dunamis power behind the stories in this book is for all Spirit-filled believers. Whether you're a brand-new Christian, or a thirty-year-old believer who's been in leadership for many years, this power is available to you now! God's calling you to ignite the dynamite now!

THE EMPOWERMENT OF THE HOLY SPIRIT

But you shall receive power when the Holy Spirit has come upon you; and you shall be witnesses to Me in Jerusalem, and in all Judea and Samaria, and to the end of the earth. (Acts 1:8)

We're not living a natural life; we're living a *supernatural* life. We've been born again and now we have this supernatural substance that dwells within us. It's the power that we received when the Holy Spirit came upon us.

Jesus said, "*But you shall receive **power** when the Holy Spirit has come upon you*" (Acts 1:8, emphasis added). The word, *power*, carries significance. In the original Koine Greek language, the word power is *dunamis.*[2] It literally means miracle-working power or explosive power. It's actually where we derive the English word *dynamite* from. Hence the title of my book, *Ignite the Dynamite*!

In Acts 1, Jesus instructs His disciples to wait until they receive this power before they are to preach the gospel to the nations. This is because the nature, and design, of dunamis power is to assist the believers in being a witness for Christ. We can still achieve results with the Word alone but we're not going to have the same impact for Jesus and His Kingdom unless we're filled with His power as described in Acts 1:8.

We receive this power when we are baptised in the Holy Spirit. The baptism of the Holy Spirit is distinct from, yet subsequent to, the born-again experience. In other words, you can be born-again yet not baptised in the Holy Spirit. This is because the baptism of the Holy Spirit is a secondary experience. It's not essential for your salvation, but it certainly is vital to your discipleship and calling. And this empowerment of the Spirit is not a one-off experience but is an on-going filling of the Spirit! As I previously stated, we can achieve results with the Word alone, but it is the baptism of the Holy Spirit that will really ignite the call of God in your life. Let's have a look at the example of Apollos.

A More Accurate Way

In Acts 18, we read that there was a believing-Jew named Apollos, who was a great teacher of the Word of God. And yet, the Bible tells us, that when Priscilla and Aquila came to him in Ephesus, they pulled him aside and explained to him the way of

God more accurately (Acts 18:26). Previously, Apollos only understood the baptism of John. We know through the gospels that John the Baptist only baptised in water. However, John proclaimed, *"I indeed baptize you with water; but One mightier than I is coming, whose sandal strap I am not worthy to loose. He will baptize you with the **Holy Spirit and fire**"* (Luke 3:16, emphasis added).

John is describing the baptism of the Holy Spirt, and this is the more accurate way explained to Apollos by Priscilla and Aquila. After that point, Apollos went on to be a major leader in the early Church. Now, let's have a look at an example from more recent times, John. G Lake, whose healing ministry exploded after receiving the baptism of the Spirit.

John G. Lake

Historically, we can read of similar occurrences where mighty ministers of God experienced a greater depth to their ministry once they had been baptised in the Holy Ghost and ignited the dynamite.

One of my heroes of the faith is John G. Lake. He would pray for the sick and sometimes see people healed, but he yearned for the empowerment and gifts of the Holy Spirit.

One afternoon, Lake and his friend were ministering to a woman suffering from inflammatory rheumatism. As Lake sat in prayer opposite the woman, he felt the presence of God come upon himself. Currents of electricity and power began to rush through his being, and he spoke in tongues for the first time. He stood, and laying the tips of his fingers upon the woman's head, streams of power flooded through her, instantly healing her!

So strong was the power flooding through Lake into the woman, that when Lake's friend took her hand, he was knocked to the floor! Lake described this event as, "a flash of dynamic power" that went through his body, through the woman's body, and into his friend's body. Later in his life, Lake described his baptism in the Holy Spirit, saying: *"And I spoke in new tongues by the power of God, and God flowed through me with a new force. Healings were more of a powerful order"*.

Just like dynamite, the English word *dynamic* is also derived from the Koine Greek word *Dunamis*. Lake recognised the manifestation of tongues, along with healing of, "A more powerful order," to have come from the dynamic power that flashed through him. Those who have been baptised in the Holy Spirit, have that same dynamic, explosive power within them, waiting to be ignited.

John G. Lake's ministry went on to bring 1,000,000 people to Christ, plant 625 Churches, and train 1,250 preachers.[3] More so, because of his healing ministry, the United States government declared his home city, Spokane, Washington, to be the healthiest city of America.

Seeking The Baptism Of The Holy Spirit

I was greatly impacted and inspired by the stories of great men and women of God, such as John G. Lake, who taught how important it was to be baptised in the Holy Spirit and be filled with this supernatural power.

I remember when I first began seeking God for this empowerment of the Spirit. Before I was married, I was living with a friend, and we had purposely rented a larger house than we needed so that we could dedicate a room to prayer. We were very disciplined; the only things that took place in that room were prayer and worship. There was no conversation with one another or anyone else. It was only conversation with God. It was in that place that I sought the Lord to be fully, without a shadow of a doubt, filled with the Holy Spirit. The word *baptism* means to be fully immersed4, and I wanted to be fully immersed by the Holy Spirit. I didn't want only to be a flickering match; I wanted to be filled with the all-consuming fire of God (Hebrews 12:29).

I was seeking God for hours and hours in prayer. One day, I was already a couple of hours into seeking Him, and I remember Him answering my prayers. By faith, I received the baptism of the Holy Spirit, and God filled me! My whole body was trembling and shaking, and I began to speak in this heavenly language. It was so supernatural; my friend and I knew that I couldn't make this up even if I tried. I was speaking words so quickly and yet so fluently. This beautiful language bubbled up and overflowed out of me. In my heart, I knew this was the book-of-Acts-encounter that I had been asking God for. This encounter lasted for hours and was coupled with crying and joyous laughter.

For the following month, the power of His presence would surge through my body like electricity, causing my body to shake and jolt physically. I didn't know what was going on; I had never experienced anything like it before. But I did know it was because of my encounter with the Holy Spirit. I wasn't expecting to have these uncontrollable surges press through me for days and even weeks on-end. It was as though I had been plugged into an electricity socket and power now flowed through me in waves. It would literally cause my body to twitch and my neck to spasm. It would happen at the most unusual times and in the most unusual places.

I was having lunch with corporate leaders from work, when suddenly I felt the electric power of God begin to stir within me. Bolts of electricity were hitting me wave after wave. This tended to happen whenever I would put my affection on God or His Word; power would surge through me. My neck started twitching and my body was spasming under the weighty presence of the Holy Spirit. My colleagues looked at me as though it was the strangest thing they had ever seen! Many people during this time in my life, would ask, 'what's wrong?' I was under the power of the Spirit, trying to explain that nothing was wrong, 'I've just encountered God!'

I used that experience as an opportunity to share Jesus with them, but to be honest, I think some of them thought I was crazy. And because this phenomenon lasted for so long, after around three or four weeks the devil started whispering in my ear and trying to twist me out of my encounter. He would try to instil fear in me; he would whisper that these surges of power had gone on for far too long and that it couldn't be God. He started to tell me that there was something *wrong* with me, that something was wrong with my nervous system.

But Jesus said His sheep will know His voice and they won't follow the voice of a stranger (John 10:4-5). I knew that I knew that this encounter was of God. In His goodness God was giving me a physical manifestation to remind me that I've got dynamite, and from that day on I will never doubt His presence and power abiding in me ever again. I'm happy to look like a fool to the world, as long as I have Jesus!

Following that encounter, just like Apollos and John G. Lake, my ministry from that point onwards exploded. I have seen many divine encounters including thousands of healings and miracles, and greatest of all, thousands of souls saved all over the world. Glory to God! His dynamite power is the same today, yesterday and forever!

In fact, this book and its contents would never have been written if it wasn't for that encounter with the Holy Spirit. A lot of the testimonies you will read in this book took place after that wild, life-changing encounter in my prayer room.

I want to finish this chapter by giving you the five biblical accounts of the baptism of the Holy Spirit in the book of Acts. If you haven't yet received the baptism of the Holy Spirit, my prayer is that this will ignite your faith to receive this dynamite power.

The Five Baptisms Of The Spirit In Acts

In the same way that salvation is received through faith, so too is the baptism of the Holy Spirit. When we're filled with the Holy Spirit, we receive access to all nine gifts of the Holy Spirit as mentioned in 1 Corinthians 12:6-7. After studying accounts of the baptism of the Holy Spirit in the book of Acts, I believe the initial evidence of the baptism of the Holy Spirit is speaking in tongues as the Spirit gives utterance. Let's look at five accounts where people were filled with the Holy Spirit for the first time:

1. The Upper-Room — Acts 2:1-4

    *When the Day of Pentecost had fully come, they were all with one accord in one place. 2 And suddenly there came a sound from heaven, as of a rushing mighty wind, and it filled the whole house where they were sitting. 3 Then there appeared to them divided tongues, as of fire, and one sat upon each of them. 4 **And they were all filled with the Holy***

Spirit and began to speak with other tongues, as the Spirit gave them utterance.

In this first account we see that the entire 120 people who were seeking God were filled with the Holy Spirit and spoke in tongues. God didn't sovereignly pick a select few. God didn't limit this supernatural manifestation to only 50 or 70 people. Every single person who was filled with the Holy Spirit began to speak in tongues as the Spirit gave utterance!

2. Paul the Apostle in Damascus - Acts 9:17-18

*17 And Ananias went his way and entered the house; and laying his hands on him he said, "Brother Saul, the Lord Jesus, who appeared to you on the road as you came, has sent me that **you may receive your sight and be filled with the Holy Spirit**." 18 Immediately there fell from his eyes something like scales, and he received his sight at once; and he arose and was baptized.*

Although the author of Acts doesn't specify on this occasion that Paul spoke in tongues, we do know from Scripture that Paul did speak in tongues. In fact, Paul would later write to the

Corinthians Church that he speaks in tongues more "than you all" (1 Corinthians 14:18).

3. Philip and the City of Samaria — Acts 8:14-17

14 Now when the apostles who were at Jerusalem heard that Samaria had received the word of God, they sent Peter and John to them, 15 who, when they had come down, prayed for them that they might receive the Holy Spirit. 16 For as yet He had fallen upon none of them. They had only been baptized in the name of the Lord Jesus. 17 Then they laid hands on them, **and they received the Holy Spirit**.

Interestingly, we know that there was some form of external manifestation when Peter and John prayed for the Samaritans to receive the Holy Spirit because the people regarded Simon Magus as a great sorcerer, and yet, he tried to buy the power of God from Peter! He recognised that the baptism of the Holy Spirit was far greater than any demonic power!

And when Simon saw that through the laying on of the apostles' hands the Holy Spirit was given, he offered them money, saying, **"Give me this power also, that anyone on whom I lay hands may receive the Holy Spirit**. (Acts 8:18-19).

4. The Household of Cornelius — Acts 10:44-46

While Peter was still speaking these words, **the Holy Spirit fell upon all those who heard the word**. *And those of the circumcision who believed were astonished, as many as came with Peter, because the gift of the Holy Spirit had been poured out on the Gentiles also.* **For they heard them speak with tongues and magnify God**.

5. Paul at Ephesus — Acts 19:6-7

And when Paul had laid hands on them, **the Holy Spirit came upon them, and they spoke with tongues and prophesied**. Now the men were about twelve in all.

On all five of these occasions, there was an outward manifestation such as speaking in tongues and the gifts of the Spirit. What follows the outpouring of the Spirit is revival and an increase in fruitful ministry.

I've also learned that the initial baptism of the Holy Spirit is not supposed to be a one-off. Even though I'm filled with the fullness of God, and I'm Spirit baptised, I hunger for God to fill me continually. The account in Acts 4 is a great example of this:

Acts 4:31

And when they had prayed, the place where they were assembled together was shaken; ***and they were all filled with the Holy Spirit****, and they spoke the word of God with boldness.*

The believers who were filled with the Holy Spirit in Acts 4 are the same believers who were Spirit baptised in Act 2! So, we know there's a continual outpouring of the Holy Spirit available for those that hunger and thirst for it.

Also, it's important to note that if the Apostles needed to wait for the empowering of the Holy Spirit to become witnesses to the ends of the earth, then how much more do we need to be filled with the Spirit and learn to ignite the dynamite that dwells within?

It is faith that ignites the dynamite. The reason this book is important to me is that faith comes by hearing and hearing by the

Word of God (Romans 10:17). I believe that as you read this book, and I unpack the scriptures along with my own testimonies, it's going to be a key ignition point to ignite the dynamite within you. My prayer is that you would get a hold of this and ignite the dynamite in every sphere of society, as a lifestyle, whenever and wherever you go.

DEMONS AND DELIVERANCE

For many Christians, the demonic realm's reality can be something far-off and distant, a spooky Bible story with little relevance for today's believers. For me the truth of demons being present and active, even in today's world, has been evident since the day I had one of my first major encounters with the spirit realm at the age of twenty-two. Around this time, as I shared in the *My Journey* chapter, our band had taken off and was playing four to five nights a week in major night clubs. I soon found that the nightclub scene was full of wickedness. I became seduced by the whole industry, including drugs, sexual immorality, and other gross sin. I also became totally sucked in by the criminal underworld. As a result, the drugs opened some serious spiritual doors to demonic entities.

Illicit mind-altering drugs, witchcraft, and demons are often closely linked with one another and have been for thousands of years. In Revelation 22:15, the Bible warns that '*sorcerers*,' or those that practice magical arts, will not inherit the Kingdom of God. Interestingly, the original Greek word for '*sorcerer*' is '*pharmakos*,' the same Greek word where we derive the words '*pharmaceuticals*,' or, '*drugs*,' from[5].

That's not to say all drugs are sorcery. Today we have medicines which can be good and helpful for the human body. However, pagans have used mind-altering drugs for thousands of years to tap into the demonic realm. And sadly, this is what I had begun to do.

I remember my first demonic experience was very freaky. I was a musician and songwriter at the time. I sat down one day, trying to write song lyrics, when suddenly something began to take over my hand and I started writing random sentences. I knew it wasn't me writing; I knew it was supernatural. This is something well known in the New Age called '*automatic writing.*' A demonic entity had taken over my body and began to use my hand to write these lyrics. After around threequarters of the way down the page of automatic writing, I remember thinking, *I wonder if this is God?*

Thoughts and memories of me as a kid and learning about Jesus in Sunday school began to flood my mind. And in that moment as I was thinking about God, the automatic writing came to a sudden stop, ending on this sentence, "Your belief in above has brought you undone."

Looking back now I can see the spiritual battle in that moment that was taking place. Even in my sin Jesus was there, fighting for me while the devil was trying to seduce me into a deeper, darker pit. It saddens me to say that this encounter did not lead me back to Jesus. In fact, this seduced me to go even deeper into the dark side. Ultimately demons want to bring about destruction and drag people into hell. However, they also try to seduce and deceive us in any way they can to lead us away from Jesus, even sometimes masquerading as an angel of light (2 Corinthians 11:14).

After this encounter, I remember beginning to believe a demonic deception. I started to believe that God and the devil both had good and evil in them. I believed that their relationship was once like a Mum and Dad. They started off well but ended in divorce. The devil was asking me to make a decision about whose side I was on.

I was so deep in my deception that it wasn't long before I was not only oppressed by demons but fully possessed by them. I was totally out of control. It got to the point that people around me, including doctors, thought I had turned into a paranoid schizophrenic. However, my condition was not a medical one but a spiritual one. No doctors or drugs could have saved me. There was only one cure for me and that was deliverance through the power of Jesus Christ!

I'll go further into my story of deliverance later in this chapter, but I want to bring some biblical understanding around the devil and his demons before I do.

What Are Demons?

Demons are wicked spirits, servants of evil, that used to have a place in Heaven as angels. In Revelation 12:7—9, the Bible describes a war breaking out in Heaven. Michael, the Archangel fought against Lucifer (satan) and his angels, casting them out of Heaven. One-third of the angels lost their place in Heaven and became what we know to be demonic spirits or demons. As much as the devil would love us to believe that he is on parr or somehow equal with God, the truth is, he is not nor has he ever been.

It's important to understand that God didn't create demons, in the sense that it wasn't His intention for demons to exist. God created all the angels, but one-third of the angels chose to follow satan in his rebellion against God. Therefore, their natures became twisted and perverse. However, God didn't will that to happen because He's not the author of evil. The author of evil is Lucifer, who isn't the only demon but is the chief demon.

The Bible describes Lucifer as once being the *"anointed Cherub,"* with *"every precious stone"* as his *"covering"* (Ezekiel 28:13-15). And just like the Cherubs that overshadowed the Ark of the Covenant (Exodus 25:18-21), his role was to be a covering for the glory of God (Ezekiel 28:13-15). This was a position of real honour. The original Hebrew word used to describe Lucifer's covering was 'מְסֻכָּה' which is transliterated into English as '*mᵉsukâ*' meaning '*garniture*' or a decorative covering6. So, Lucifer was clothed with every precious stone imaginable, and on top of this, he covered the glory of the Lord.

I believe that the glory of the Lord would reflect off Lucifer's covering, causing phenomenal beams of light and colours to emanate from the precious stones. One of the only Earthly things I can think of to relate this too would be the most vibrant rainbow you could possibly witness. Beams of light that cause the most amazing spectrum of colour. But to be honest, there's nothing on the Earth that can compare to the glory of God on display.

As the angels would gaze upon Lucifer, he began to think too highly of himself and to believe that it was his own glory they were seeing. Instead of giving praise back to God, Lucifer began to fall to pride and think himself equal to God. He forgot that it was the glory of God that caused him to shine, and it was God who created him in that fashion.

The Bible tells us that Lucifer was perfect until iniquity was found in him, *"You were perfect in your ways from the day you were created, Till iniquity was found in you"* (Ezekiel 28:15). Then, through his pride and free-will, Lucifer led a third of the angels in a rebellion against God. This was devastating for all creation as it was the beginning of evil. At this point, Lucifer became the devil, the father of lies (John 8:44) and the author of evil, whose mission is to kill, steal and destroy (John 10:10).

Now that we know what demons are, let's take a look at what they do. One of the ways that demons try to bring about their destruction is through human vessels. They look for a vessel that they can influence, and even try to possess, to bring about their work of destruction.

Oppression vs Possession

Over the years I have often been asked, what is the difference between demons oppressing and possessing someone?

There is certainly a difference. Simply put, I describe oppression as an external attack on the mind, will, emotions or body, of a human. However, to be possessed means that the devil has taken control of the inner man, or spirit, of a person. To be possessed means that the demon, or demons, have taken up residence inside of your spirit. Let me unpack this a little more.

Oppression from demons is something every human will face, whether they realise the source or not; Christians and nonChristians alike.

Demons are entities in the unseen realm that try to make life hell for the people on Earth. Their wicked role is to bring oppression, which can come in many different forms such as depression, anxiety, fear, confusion, sickness, and even suicidal thoughts— to name a few.

This is why Christians need to know their authority in Christ. We need to know how to combat the devil's schemes over us. The Bible says, *"Submit to God, resist the devil and he will flee"* (James 4:7). The truth is that demons are afraid of real Christians who know their authority in Christ.

The Bible also teaches us in Ephesians that we can take up the shield of faith and extinguish the fiery darts from the devil. The devil tries to trespass and oppress Christians, but really demons have no authority over us. They must flee. The devil is under our feet. Jesus has already destroyed the power of darkness and, *"He who is in you is greater than he who is in the world"* (1 John 4:4).

When it comes to demonic *possession*, only a non-Christian needs to fear this. It normally occurs after someone continues in dark, on-going sin. When I became possessed by demons it was after I began to practice the dark-arts, along with drugs and gross sexual sin. I remember yielding my will to these demonic spirits and they took over my spirit. Because of sin I gave them authority and an open door to take over and possess me. This, for me, was much more destructive and dangerous than other previous outward oppressive attacks.

Christians, however, need not fear possession. Human beings are made up of three different parts: body, soul, and spirit. When we become born-again, our spirits are made brand-new! The Bible says, *"Therefore, if anyone is in Christ, he is a new creation; old things have passed away; behold, all things have become new"* (2 Corinthians 5:17). The Holy Spirit has fused Himself to our own spirits, and now we are brand new creations! So, a demon cannot possess a Christian's spirit.

The only possible way for a demon to gain control of a Christian's spirit is if that person has decided to continue or go back into habitual, unrepentant sin and if they have decided to leave their faith. By grieving the Holy Spirit, and by pushing Him out of the recesses of their heart, they forfeit their salvation and give legal rights to demonic entities to possess their inner-being.

However, someone who is walking in the ways of God has nothing to fear. Nothing can separate us from the love of God (Romans 8:37-39), no devil in hell, no principality over any nation, no demonic spirit can possess a born-again, spirit-filled Christian.

Deliverance In Salvation

Now that we have looked at what demons are and what they do, let's get to the most important part of the chapter. How do we cast demons out and see people delivered?

Firstly, the best way to see someone delivered is to get them saved. The word salvation in the original Koine Greek is *Soteria*7. It literally means healed, delivered, and forgiven. More specifically, it's referring to physical healing, spiritual deliverance from demonic spirits, and forgiveness of sin. When the Holy Spirit comes into the life of a brand-new believer, demons can't hang around. They are afraid of Jesus. Sometimes deliverance can happen without much fuss upon salvation, but sometimes demons may try to resist what is happening. It's also important to get someone saved when being delivered from demonic spirits. If the person doesn't get filled with the Holy Spirit, the Bible teaches that seven more wicked spirits will return to the person, and they will be even worse off than before.

> *When an unclean spirit goes out of a man, he goes through dry places, seeking rest, and finds none.* **Then he says, 'I will return to my house from which I came.'** *And when he comes, he finds it empty, swept, and put in order. Then he goes and takes with him seven other spirits more wicked than himself, and they enter and dwell there;* **and the last state of that man is worse than the first.** *So shall it also be with this wicked generation.* (Matthew 12:43-45).

When I gave my life to Jesus, I received a major deliverance from many demons and demonic strongholds. However, it was a process before I received full deliverance. It wasn't until I confessed my sin to my Mum that the final devil came out of my life.

As I mentioned earlier in the chapter, I was into some very evil and wicked stuff. I developed a love and curiosity for crime and the underworld, and I was particularly drawn to drugs. I also hated the police.

I remember when I first tried to confess this to my Mum, the demon wouldn't let me. It was a spirit of lawlessness that had its hooks in my life, pulling the strings and controlling me. It bound my mouth closed so that I couldn't speak. It was a pretty crazy experience for my Mum and me.

Mum called my Aunty because she had some experience in deliverance. My Aunty prayed for me over the phone and the devil was cast out.

It was the confession of my sin that brought the demon into the light. The book of James speaks about the importance of confessing our sins to one another and not just to God, *"Confess your trespasses to one another, and pray for one another, that you may be healed. The effective, fervent prayer of a righteous man avails much"* (James 5:16).

Confession was key to my deliverance and so too was my Aunty's understanding of her authority in Christ. She simply had faith, ignited the dynamite, and the devil had no choice but to leave my life.

The Gadarean Man

Jesus cast out many demons in His three years of public ministry. One of the most famous and notable accounts was the *'Gadarean man.'*

When Jesus went to the country of the Gadareans, He came across a man with an unclean spirit. In fact, this man had a legion of spirits possessing him. He was bound by many demons, so much so, he had supernatural strength. The people in the region would try and chain him up because they were so scared of him, but they couldn't keep him bound. The man would break the shackles and the chains with his demonic supernatural strength. And so it seemed, nothing in the natural could stop this man.

The only answer was the power of the Holy Spirit. The town discovered this when Jesus came along and cast the demons out of the man.

The interesting part of this story is that Jesus spoke to the demons. The demons didn't want to be cast out into the dry places again. They had asked Jesus to allow them to go into the swine and Jesus granted their request.

When I first read this story, I was thinking, *Why would Jesus even care about what they wanted? Why did He send them into the swine?*

After a few years of thinking about this, meditating on it, and praying about it, I realised Jesus used this as a sign and wonder to the town. The Gadarean man was notorious throughout the town as someone who had supernatural strength, lived in the tombs, and was naked. He was known as a crazy, crazy man. And Jesus comes along; He casts the demons out of the man and into the pigs. Once those demons entered the pigs, they violently ran into the water and drowned.

Now, those who were caring for the pigs at the time witnessed all of this take place. They saw the Gadarean man come back into his right mind, and they saw the spirits go into the pigs. These witnesses knew without a shadow of a doubt that Jesus had just done something supernatural. This caused those who fed the pigs to flee; they were so afraid because what was happening was so freaky. They went and told the whole city what had happened and because the Gadarean man was notorious, this was a sign and wonder to an entire town about the power of God.

That's what happens when we cast out demons; not only does the person get free, but it's a sign and wonder that causes people to marvel at the power of God.

That's a wonderful example of deliverance and it also shows us that you can't combat demonic power with a natural solution. Fighting demons cannot be done by might or by human power. It can only be done through the power of the Holy Spirit. Only by the dunamis miracle working power that abides in Spirit-filled Christians.

Now, we shall dive into unpacking one of the most important keys in ministering deliverance to people.

Prayer And Fasting

Learning how to cast out demons was integrated into the discipleship journey of the disciples of Jesus. We see an example of this in Mark 9, where the father of a boy tormented by a demonic spirit asked the disciples to cast the demon out of his son. The disciples couldn't do it and so the father brought the boy to Jesus, and Jesus set him free.

This wasn't because the disciples didn't have the power or authority to cast out the demon. The disciples did have the power and the authority, and they were learning to minister just like Jesus. When they asked Jesus why they weren't able to cast the demon out, Jesus taught them that, *"This kind can come out by nothing but prayer and fasting"* (Mark 9:29). In other words, Jesus was saying that this one comes out by faith, and you need faith to ignite the dynamite, and if you've got doubt, then you don't have faith.

When we pray and fast, we realign our focus onto God, and in doing so, it removes the doubt in our hearts. We only need a mustard seed of faith to get the job done. We see Jesus teaching the disciples the importance of prayer and fasting because it was the mandate of the twelve to cast out demons. In this next section, we will unpack how that mandate was never intended to only be for the twelve disciples but for all Spirit-filled believers.

All Believers Should Cast Out Demons

In the gospels, we clearly see that Jesus didn't limit His power and authority to a select few. In fact, in Luke 10, Jesus expanded His team of missionaries from the twelve Apostles to include seventy disciples, also giving them the power to cast out demons. We see this in Luke 10:17, when the seventy disciples returned to Jesus, *"Then the seventy returned with joy, saying, "Lord, even the demons are subject to us in Your name."*

It's interesting to note that in response to this, Jesus did in fact affirm their authority over demons, but He also reminded them that their joy should be found in their names being written in the lamb's book of life.

> *And He said to them, "I saw Satan fall like lightning from heaven. Behold,* **I give you the authority to trample on serpents and scorpions, and over all the power of the enemy,** *and nothing shall by any means hurt you. Nevertheless do not rejoice in this, that the spirits are subject to you,* **but rather rejoice because your names are written in heaven.** *"* (Luke 10:18-20, emphasis added).

We clearly see here that authority to trample demonic powers belongs to those whose names are written in heaven. Amazingly, this wasn't only true for the twelve or the seventy disciples, but Jesus made it inclusive of all those who would believe in Him. In Mark 16:15-18, Jesus says:

> *"Go into all the world and preach the gospel to every creature. He who believes and is baptized will be saved;*

but he who does not believe will be condemned. And these signs will follow those who believe: In My name they will cast out demons; they will speak with new tongues; they will take up serpents; and if they drink anything deadly, it will by no means hurt them; they will lay hands on the sick, and they will recover. (Emphasis added).

Jesus says that a sign of someone who believes is that they will cast out demons in His name. In Matthew 28:16-20, Jesus instructed the twelve disciples to go into all the world and create new disciples, teaching them to, *"observe all things that I have commanded you."* First, Jesus sent out the twelve Apostles, and they cast out demons. Then He sent-out the seventy disciples, and they cast out demons. And now, He has extended His commission to all new believers. It's a disciple cycle, and casting out demons is a part of that discipleship lifestyle.

The necessity to cast out demons hasn't changed. If anything, the Bible says the devil knows his time is short (Revelation 12:12). He's causing even more damage and destruction in a desperate attempt to destroy as many people as he can. It's imperative that we understand the importance of casting out demons more today than ever. Being discipled in igniting the dynamite and stepping into our authority as believers to cast out demons is very important. This is why I'm excited about this book, and this chapter in particular, because we need people to understand the importance of casting out demons.

Casting out demons can be really simple; just speak to the demonic spirit and command it to get out! We don't need to be afraid or freaked out because it's the Holy Spirit working through us to remove the demonic entity.

One of the best ways to learn how to cast out demons is to watch someone do it. I'm thankful for my friend Ben Fitzgerald. As a new Christian, I would watch him cast out demons on the street! In my early years of faith, we saw countless demons cast out.

One of my favourite stories of deliverance took place on the streets of Frankston.

One day, Ben and I were out looking for an opportunity to share our faith. The area was notorious for its crime rate and drug and alcohol abuse. Ben and I would constantly hit the streets with our hearts burning to share the gospel, pray for the sick, and cast out devils. We were learning to ignite the dynamite and were eager to demonstrate the power of God.

This particular afternoon, we decided to head down to the beach with our Bibles and spend some time in prayer. On our way there, we came across a group of guys sitting at a table drinking. They looked like rough guys, they were covered in tattoos and looked like they had been drinking heavily with beer bottles and cheap cask wine around the table. You could tell these weren't the sort of guys to mess with. Maybe for some people this sort of scene would be intimidating or off putting. They were certainly intoxicated which might make them seem harder to approach. However, Ben and I knew these sorts of guys were the ones who we really needed to reach. Jesus said that He didn't come for the righteous or for those who think they have it all together, but He came for the sick (Mark 2:17). And these guys were certainly sick. They were desperate for God and didn't know it. They were bound by demons and bound by alcoholism.

So, we went up to these rough looking guys and asked them if we could sit down at the table with them for a chat. They saw the Bibles in our hands and asked, "What do you have there? What's that book?"

We said, "It's the Bible. Is it alright if we talk to you for a little bit about the Bible and Jesus?"

We ended up sharing with these guys our stories and our testimonies. We shared with them how we had come out of drug addiction, alcoholism, and being bound by demons. In the early stages of this conversation what we said was received well. They were actually a little friendlier than they looked. There was one guy in particular who really stood out to us. We found out later that he had just come out of prison for manslaughter. We didn't know the details of the manslaughter, but it was clear he was a rough guy. As we were chatting, one of his friends accidentally knocked his last beer bottle out of his hand and it smashed all over the floor.

The guy just lost it.

All of his friends didn't even wait to see what would happen next. They knew how crazy he was, they leapt from their chairs and bolted. Ben and I were left alone with this enraged guy, thinking: *What's going on?*

The guy stands up. Ben and I stand up. And the guy pulls out a knife and slashes out at us. We could see the hatred in his eyes; this wasn't a normal human reaction, it was demonic.

The guy swings his knife at us and misses, and in that moment, Ben says, "In the name of Jesus I bind the devil! I bind the spirit of murder that is over you, in Jesus' name!" (See Matthew 18:18).

As the words "In Jesus' name" came out of Ben's mouth, it was as though something snapped within the guy. All of his violent hostility instantly froze, Ben had bound the demon in the name of Jesus!

Ben continued, "And I command you in Jesus' name, to put the knife in the bin!"

Just behind the table where we had been sitting, there was a big public bin. It was really freaky because we could see this guy had no idea what was going on. All of a sudden, he obeys the command and places the knife in the bin! And from that point onward, we were able to share the full gospel with him and cast the devil out of his life. All his mates were long gone by this stage, it was just him and us. Of his own accord he got down on his knees and raised his hands, with tears streaming down his face and in his own words, he began to ask Jesus to forgive him. We helped guide him in prayer as he asked Jesus to come into his life and asked for forgiveness for sin. That was when we learned of how he had just come out of prison.

We then took him down to the local Church to meet the Pastor and encouraged him to remain plugged in and planted in the local

Church. He was doing well and continued on with his faith in Jesus Christ and soon after that encounter, he passed away. This made us grateful that we didn't allow intimidation to stop the gospel from being preached; we got our chance to share the gospel with him and Jesus saved him before he died.

Since my time learning from Ben on the streets, I've now literally seen thousands of demons come out of people all over the world. My prayer is that this chapter will fire you up to step out and pray for those that are demonically bound.

DISCIPLED IN HEALING

Jesus intended divine health and healing to be a part of the normal Christian life. In fact, divine healing and health are woven into the very fabric of the atonement. But how do we see the sick healed? How do we live in divine health?

This topic of divine healing has been something that I have been drawn to right from the very early stages of my Christianity. I've researched, studied, and practised divine healing for more than ten thousand hours over the past seventeen years. During this time, I have literally seen God heal thousands of people all over the world.

I remember my passion starting as a new Christian getting a hold of the *God's General's* DVD series and watching them on repeat for hours a day. I was being totally inspired by people like Jack Coe, Katheryn Kuhlman, Smith Wigglesworth, John G. Lake, and A.A. Allan, to name just a few. These guys were Generals of their time who knew their God and did great exploits (Daniel 11:32). Around this time, I decided to make it my life's mission to live this way. Just like these Generals I wanted to fully yield my will to seeking first the Kingdom of God and His righteousness (Matthew 6:33). I decided to dedicate my life to being a part of another great awakening and what I believe to be the last end-time revival and out-pouring before Jesus comes back.

Let's get into this chapter by starting with what I believe is the most important key to igniting the dynamite for healing.

Faith

Faith is essential to the Christian life. We can have miracle working power dwelling within us, we can have dynamite, but without faith the wick is wet and the dynamite lays dormant. Faith is like an ignition, or a spark, that ignites the dynamite. It is through faith that we access divine health and divine healing. Through faith, all believers can actually release healing to others! The Bible says in Mark 16:15,

> *And He said to them, "Go into all the world and preach the gospel to every creature. He who believes and is baptized will be saved; but he who does not believe will be condemned. And these signs will follow those who **believe**: In My name they will cast out demons; they will speak with new tongues; they will take up serpents; and if they drink*

anything deadly, it will by no means hurt them; ***they will lay hands on the sick, and they will recover.*** (Emphasis added).

The Bible also says in James 5:15, *"And **the prayer of faith will save the sick**, and the Lord will raise him up. And if he has committed sins, he will be forgiven"* (emphasis added). It is the prayer of faith that will see the sick healed!

So, how do we have faith? The Bible makes it really clear, *"So then faith comes by hearing, and hearing by the word of God"* (Romans 10:17). In other words, to pray the prayer of faith we need to know it is in His Word so we can pray according to His will. My heart is to equip believers to live every day fully in faith, knowing that they have the authority and the ability already in them to destroy the works of the devil. Sickness is certainly a part of the works of the devil. The prayer of faith is what ignites the dynamite to destroy sickness! But before I go further into this subject of faith and supernatural healing, I first want to quickly point out that our bodies are a temple of the Holy Spirit (1 Corinthians 6:19) and it's important that we steward and look after our temple properly. A balanced healthy life and healthy diet is very important. And this lifestyle can help prevent sickness and disease. God's pretty amazing; our bodies can be healed and stay healthy through certain foods that God has created; and of course a lifestyle of exercise has been proven to be a great preventative of sickness and disease. However, having said all this, it's also important for us to understand that even the healthiest person in the world still needs to understand the concept of faith for divine health and divine healing.

It's God's Will To Heal

We don't need to doubt whether it is God's will to heal the sick because God has made it really clear in His Word. Isaiah 53:5 says, *"But He was wounded for our transgressions, He was bruised for our iniquities; The chastisement for our peace was upon Him,* ***And by His stripes we are healed****"* (Emphasis added).

Psalm 103:2-3 also says, *"Bless the Lord, O my soul, And forget not all His benefits: Who forgives all your iniquities,* ***Who heals all your diseases****"* (Emphasis added). That's the Word of God, and these are just some of the many scriptures that reveals God's heart and will for divine healing.

We stand on the promise of His Word and pray in faith. The prayer of faith is birthed from knowing God's Word and thereby knowing His will. We look at the life of Jesus because He is the express image and perfect example of God the Father (Hebrews 1:3). When we read the Gospels we can see that everywhere Jesus went He healed the sick. Why? Because that is the will of the Father. I also know that the will of God has not, and does not, change! The Bible says, *"Jesus Christ is the same yesterday, today, and forever"* (Hebrews 13:8).

I remember receiving this revelation as a new Christian studying the Gospels. With this revelation stirring in my heart, I couldn't help but go out and begin to co-labour with Jesus to see people saved, healed, and delivered.

When I first began to step out in faith to see people supernaturally healed, I must have prayed for at least 100 people and only saw a headache healed! For a time, I felt discouraged, and I felt the temptation to give up. Yet, I had experienced for myself God's explosive power to heal. He radically saved me and healed me from a life of drug and alcohol addiction. More so, the Bible is full of miracles, and I knew that if I was going to claim to believe the Bible, then I couldn't deny God is a miracle-working God.

I began to dive deep into the scriptures and meditate on His Word. As I've mentioned above, the Bible says, *"so then faith comes by hearing, and hearing by the word of God*" (Romans 10:17). I knew that if I was going to see the sick healed, I needed to grow in my faith. And that's the same lesson Jesus taught His disciples!

In Matthew 17:14-21, there was a man whose son was demon-possessed. This possession was so intense that the demons would cause the boy to have seizures, foam at the mouth, and even try to get the boy to kill himself. The man took his son to the disciples of Jesus to be healed, but the boy remained possessed.

When the man saw Jesus, he told Him of his son's condition and how the disciples could not cast the demon out of the boy. Jesus exclaimed, "*O faithless and perverse generation, how long shall I be with you? How long shall I bear with you? Bring him here to Me*" (Matthew 17:17).

Then Jesus commanded the demons out of the boy, and the boy was completely healed and restored!

Later, the disciples asked Jesus privately why they couldn't cast the demon out. Jesus said:

> *Because of your unbelief; for assuredly, I say to you, if you have faith as a mustard seed, you will say to this mountain, 'Move from here to there,' and it will move; and nothing will be impossible for you.* **However, this kind does not go**

out except by prayer and fasting. (Matthew 17:20-21, emphasis added).

I love that Jesus didn't shy away from giving His disciples loving truth. He taught them how to heal the sick and cast out demons, He was also correcting them, telling them their thinking was faithless and twisted. They weren't thinking in faith, so Jesus gave them a very important key; *prayer and fasting!* It was actually this particular passage of teaching by Jesus that inspired me in the following story.

It was early days in my Christianity, and I was seeking breakthrough in the area of healing the sick. I was hungry for the dynamite power of God to flow through me and impact those around me. At this point of my journey, I had only seen some miracles take place here and there. And of course, as you read in my journey, my life is a walking miracle! But I hadn't yet experienced a notable miracle where I personally laid my hands on the sick and saw them recover. I had witnessed a few sparks now and then, but I sensed God wanted to ignite His explosive power in my life. As I mentioned, I read the words of Jesus in Matthew 17 and I became inspired. I knew what I needed to do!

I took annual leave from my job, purchased a slab of water and dedicated a week to prayer and fasting. What a wonderful time being with the Lord! Even though, I struggled in the flesh sometimes, it was a beautiful time of drawing close to the heart of God. By the end of the week, miracles were at the forefront of my mind. I was bursting at the seams for the opportunity to pray for the sick. On the final day of my fast, I needed to go to my local bank, and I was hoping to meet someone that I could pray for as I went about my business. When I entered the bank, my eyes were drawn to a man who had his arm in a sling. As it turned out, I recognised the guy from my pre-Christian, nightclub days! I struck up a conversation with him and he started telling me about his injury. He had broken his collarbone while mountain bike racing. The doctors had told him it would take seven weeks to heal, but he was only three weeks in and he was in an immense amount of pain.

I asked him if I could pray for him. He responded that he had heard I had become "church-ee" and agreed. I put my hand upon him and commanded for his shoulder and arm to be made fully well in the name of Jesus! My old friend looked taken aback; he thought I was going to go home and say a nice little prayer before bed. He wasn't expecting that I would pray for him right there in the middle of the bank!

After I prayed for him, I gave him my phone number and carried on with my banking. The very next day, I received a text message from him. There were several swear words of shock that I don't want to repeat in this book, and a message that read, "I don't know what you did, but last night was the first night in weeks that I slept like a baby and today I have no pain!".

Faith bubbled up within me! I remembered that the Word of God says there is life and death in the tongue (Proverbs 18:21), and so I continued to declare healing over him. I responded to his text, "I want you to know, it wasn't me who healed you. It was Jesus! Watch what happens; you're going to be completely healed and will be back racing your mountain bike!"

Three days later, he texts me again— his collarbone was completely healed, and He was back to racing his mountain bike!

After that experience, the floodgates of healing burst open and something shifted. I felt as though I had been awakened. Miracles weren't just a hopeful theory for me anymore; they became the standard of expectation. And after that first miracle, many more followed! In fact, it got to the point where I was more surprised if someone didn't get healed than if they did!

The Atonement

Jesus paid the ultimate price so that we could see divine healing and live in divine health. The Bible makes it clear that physical healing is in the atonement of Christ. Isaiah 53:5 says, *"But He was wounded for our transgressions, He was bruised for our iniquities; The chastisement for our peace was upon Him,* ***And by His stripes we are healed***" (emphasis added). Over the years I've noticed many Christians have no problem understanding and having faith in the fact that Jesus was wounded and crucified on the cross for the forgiveness and removal of our transgressions. Yet sometimes, believers forget or perhaps don't recognise, that the same Isaiah 53 passage says, *by His stripes we are healed.* God does not want us to forget and miss out on this benefit that Jesus paid for on the cross.

Some try to argue that Isaiah was not talking about physical healing, but this is incorrect. The word for *healed* in the original Hebrew language is *Rapha.* And it literally means "to cure" or to "mend"[8], and it certainly has, but not limited to, the implication of physical healing. In fact, one of God's names is *Jehovah Rapha.* Exodus 15:26 says,

*"If you diligently heed the voice of the Lord your God and do what is right in His sight, give ear to His commandments and keep all His statutes, **I will put none of the diseases on you** which I have brought on the Egyptians. **For I am the Lord who heals [Rapha] you.*** (Emphasis added).

As you can see, the immediate context here is physical healing.

If you do a study on the word Rapha, you will find it is used over sixty times in the Old Testament. The majority of this word's usage directly describes physical healing! Although sometimes it can be used to describe a physician (Jeremiah 8:22), and in other cases it can be used to describe a metaphorical healing, such as the healing of backsliding (Jeremiah 3:22 & Hosea 14:4) or the healing of the waters (2 Kings 2:21-22 and Ezekiel 47:8-9). Finally, let me show you something in the New Testament that will leave you without a shadow of doubt that physical healing is in the atonement.

Matthew brings his commentary on Isaiah 53:5 and makes the intended definition absolutely clear. This is why studying the Bible in its entirety is so important because often scripture will interpret scripture. When we study the Bible this way, we are left with no doubt or room for our own private interpretation (2 Peter 1:20). Matthew 8:16-17 says:

> *When evening had come, they brought to Him many who were demon-possessed. And He cast out the spirits with a word, and healed all who were sick, that it might be fulfilled which was spoken by Isaiah the prophet, saying, "He Himself took our **infirmities** And bore our **sicknesses**."* (Emphasis added).

As you can see, the Word of God explicitly reveals that physical healing is within the atonement. This is important to understand because, as we have stated, faith comes by hearing, and hearing by the Word of God (Romans 10:17).

Our Authority

When I first started praying for the sick, I didn't understand the authority God had given me as a believer. I was still learning that disciples of Christ have authority over sickness and the power of the enemy. But then one day something really cool happened that showed me I had the authority to release God's explosive power!

It was not long after experiencing my first real breakthrough miracle, with the collarbone, that I met a man on the streets from Botswana, Africa. It was an amazing divine appointment! I shared the gospel with him and he gave his life to Jesus!

That following Sunday I drove to his house and picked him up to take him to Church. After the service, I remember asking him how he enjoyed the service and if he had any questions about the preaching. I noticed that as I was talking with him, he would turn his head around to face his right ear toward me. I wondered if he had any problems with his hearing, so I asked him why he was turning his right ear toward me. It turned out, that he was stone-cold deaf in his left ear since the age of 8 years old! He was now in his 20s and had gone most of his life only hearing through one ear!

I knew in that moment that God wanted me to take authority over the situation. I knew that instead of asking God to heal him, I needed to command the ear to open with authority! I cupped my hands around his left ear and I shouted twice, "Open! Open!"

What followed was one of the most amazing things I have ever seen in my life. Tears of joy began to stream down his face as he declared, "I can hear! I can hear!"

In that moment, I fully understood the authority we have in Christ Jesus! The Jesus that we represent is the name above every other name! I finally understood the authority I have as an ambassador of Christ (2 Corinthians 5:20). I recognised that He has already given me His power, and it doesn't come and go! It's the Acts 1:8 dynamite power that abides within me. I realised: I am His son and I am His ambassador!

From then onwards, I stopped doubting whether God could heal the sick and I stopped questioning whether it was His will. Instead, I stepped into my authority and began to command sickness to get out of people's bodies! It wasn't my power doing it, it was the power of Jesus flowing through me! I started to realise that I don't need to wait for a word from God to heal the sick. The Bible has already told me to go lay hands and heal the sick. I realised that I don't have to beg God to heal the sick. He had already said yes! He had already given me His miracle-working power; I just had to ignite it!

Like I said earlier, the Bible says that we are ambassadors of Christ (2 Corinthians 5:20). The role of an ambassador is a vital role, even in the earthly sense. An ambassador has been granted power and authority to take action on behalf of their government or king they represent. That is the human understanding of the earthly role of an ambassador.

However, it is the same in the Kingdom of Heaven! The Bible calls us ambassadors for Christ. That means we have been given power and authority to take action on behalf of the King! We have been commissioned by the King and as ambassadors we have been fully equipped with power and authority to see our mission fulfilled.

The Apostle Peter understood this authority when he came across the lame man featured in Acts 3:1-8. The lame man wasn't in a place of faith, nor was he even asking for healing, he was begging for money. When Peter and John crossed his path Peter said to the lame man: *I don't have any money but what I do have I give to you in the name of Jesus!* At that moment, Peter commanded the man to rise up and walk in the name of the Lord Jesus Christ! He didn't pray a soft prayer. It wasn't, *hey God is it your will this time?* And it wasn't, *God can you please heal this man?*

Peter understood his authority! He knew that he was an ambassador for Christ! Peter called upon the name of His King to enforce the King's edict— and the lame man walked! Peter was following the commission of Jesus Christ, just as we should today.

This doesn't mean Peter was the source of the healing. In fact, he constantly pointed back to Jesus and said that it was Christ who was doing the healing. It was the miracle-working dynamite that had been given to him, and he knew how to ignite it.

Finally, my prayer is that this chapter stirs you greatly to go after seeing the sick healed. Divine healing is a huge part of what it looks like to ignite the dynamite. Everywhere Jesus went He healed the sick. And now He's calling you to step out and do the same thing!

IT'S FOR ALL BELIEVERS

It is so important that all Spirit-filled believers understand that they can ignite the dynamite. Whether you're a brand-new Christian or seasoned in the faith, your faith in Jesus has qualified you to ignite the dynamite and live like Jesus. Over the years I have found that it is sometimes the new Christians that learn how to ignite the dynamite quicker. I've seen a pattern of Christians being mentored or discipled in wrong thinking, so rather than having child-like faith, like a new Christian, the more seasoned Christians can sometimes be bound in doubt and false doctrine around things that are opposite to what the Bible says. The Bible warns of people who have a form of godliness but deny the power (2 Timothy 3:5). Sometimes, to teach people faith we first have to unravel the doubt that comes through wrong teaching and wrong doctrine. I hope that this book will help me do that very thing.

My mentor and contributor to this book, Frank, is a great example of this. When he first got saved, he opened his bible to the book of Acts and simply believed he could do the same thing. Frank was praying for the sick and seeing them healed! But then, some well-meaning Pastors and bible Teachers tried to teach him reasons why some people won't get healed. This caused him to waver in his faith and as a result he didn't see as many people healed anymore. Praise God he's back on track again now and firing on all cylinders! You will hear more on this from Frank later in his chapter.

As you will discover in this book, God was able to use me powerfully even in the early days of being saved. Now my heart, as a five-fold ministry leader, is to see every believer equipped to be used by God in the same way.

In my early days of Church planting, we would send brandnew believers out onto the streets to share the gospel, heal the sick, and cast out devils. We'd send them out with a team captain who was a seasoned believer, but the idea was to release them to practise what they were learning through discipleship.

One particular lady who was a brand-new Christian, had a lot of fear. She even struggled to talk with us, let alone share her new faith with strangers. However, we had been discipling her and praying with her and she was set free from her fear. She decided to go out with the street team and put into practice what she had been learning about the righteous being as bold as lions (Proverbs 28:1).

On an outreach she saw an elderly lady in a wheel-chair who was with her family. Pushing through all fear that waged war against her boldness, she walked up to the family and said, "Excuse me, could I please pray for the lady?"

The family responded, "Look, she's old. She's had a stroke and hasn't had feeling in her left side for years. We do believe in God, and we've prayed for her ourselves, so don't worry about it. But thank you."

But this brand-new Christian who was breaking the power of fear in her life, felt in her heart to press-in and ask again. She boldly asked, "Please can I pray? I believe Jesus will heal her."

The family reluctantly agreed. She laid her hands on the woman in the wheelchair and said a real simple prayer, knowing that the family were counting the seconds for her to leave. Before she left, she gave them our Church's card and asked them to please contact us if the woman's condition changed. That was on Saturday.

On Monday I had the Church phone, and I received a phone call from one of the family members who said, "I want to thank you so much, a lady from your Church prayed for my Mum who had had a stroke two years ago. For the past two years, she has had no feeling her left side. But since this lady's prayer all the feeling has returned to her body! Once again, she can move by herself and even dress herself!"

That was a notable miracle from a brand-new Christian who overcame fear and had simple faith! The power of God is for everyone, not just for ministers, the twelve Apostles, or even seasoned Christians. God wants to use all believers.

It's For All Believers

Something that is commonly taught but is very wrong, is that the supernatural power of God was only given to the twelve Apostles for the establishment of the Church. We'll go deeper on this cessationist belief in the next chapter. The truth is, God anointed not only the twelve Apostles but also another seventy disciples, teaching them to heal the sick and cast out devils (Luke 10:1-12). Then, in the Great Commission, Jesus instructs the Apostles to teach all believers to follow all things Jesus had taught them (Matthew 28:20). This includes not only instruction in right Christian living, but also discipleship in igniting the dynamite. Jesus never intended for the power to be for a certain chosen few; He wants every believer in every nation to be discipled in how to operate in the supernatural.

Already Qualified

Over the years, I've had to help people unravel the mindset that they need to be behind a pulpit as a leader of a Church before they can operate in signs and wonders.

I think it's amazing when someone wants to become a Church leader, Pastor, or a five-fold minister. It's wonderful when someone feels called to Bible College. I would encourage anyone who is called to any of those good things to pursue them. The Bible says, *"This is a faithful saying: If a man desires the position of a bishop, he desires a good work"* (1 Timothy 3:1). So we definitely want people to be inspired to pursue the call of God on their lives.

At the same time, if we're not careful, we may think what qualifies us to share our faith and operate in the miraculous is our external recognition. I've seen it firsthand; people chase after a degree, or a position in leadership, hoping the miraculous would be ignited in their lives. But the truth is you were qualified to ignite the dynamite the day you were born again and filled with the Spirit.

Not A Spectator

It is an incredible honour to preach behind the pulpit. It is an esteemed opportunity to be able to equip the saints in God's Church at such a time as this. However, I also understand that we're not going to see the world saved from behind a pulpit. Ultimately, the job of the person behind the pulpit is to equip the saints for lifestyle evangelism and discipleship.

I often like to use the analogy of a football game. Now, I'm from Australia and we love football. We have a game called Australian Rules Football, and I've played football for several years. I understand how football works, and when teaching on this topic, I would often bring a parallel between the coach's address and what happens out on the field.

In a football team the coach is essential. The team is not going to perform well if they don't have excellent coaching. However, what happens in the coach's address to the team is not actually going to win the game. It will certainly help; what happens out on the field is what wins the game.

It is the same with Christianity; I consider what happens on a Sunday morning as the metaphorical coach's address. The coach is firing up the saints. The coach is teaching them, equipping them, and getting them ready for the game. The coach prepares the saints for their week and for their everyday lives. Equipping them to destroy the works of the devil, operate in the ministry of reconciliation (2 Corinthians 5:18), and flow in miracles, signs, and wonders.

We need the coaches. We need Pastors and Church leaders. The pulpit is important; the coach's half-time address is important. But what really matters is what happens out on the field.

It's also important for Christians to understand that none of us are called to be spectators, sitting way back in the nosebleeds, criticising the Church from our seats. No; the coach's address isn't given to the spectators. Every single Christian is called to roll up their sleeves and get into the game.

The truth is, no matter what your function in the Church, everyone has the same Spirit that raised Jesus from the dead abiding within them. That means everyone can operate in the dynamite power, whether you're an Apostle, serving in the helps ministry, or a regular Churchgoer. We all have the same power and it's the same faith that ignites it. Saying *yes* to Him is what qualifies us to be filled with the Spirit and to operate in signs and wonders.

Act 6 is a great example of this. The Apostles selected seven people to help serve in the hospitality department. One of the seven was Stephen. Stephen's role in the public Church meeting was not preaching behind the pulpit; neither was he praying for the sick or prophesying. His role was to simply help administer food to the widows. He would go to the market to buy food and then bring it back to be distributed amongst the widows. But even though he wasn't an Apostle or a five-fold ministry leader, we read that he still performed signs and wonders in the marketplace. He understood that he had the same dynamite in him as the Apostles and every other believer, *"And Stephen, full of faith and power, did great wonders and signs among the people"* (Acts 6:8).

I hope that after reading this book, every believer will begin to ignite the dynamite. No matter who you are or where you are, whether you are in a Church service, at the next Awakening stadium event, or going about your normal day-to-day life. God's heart is that everyone will begin to ignite the dynamite and that miracles will begin to break out everywhere.

CESSATIONISM

In my early years of salvation, I didn't understand the differences between denominations and their doctrinal beliefs. I was quite naive; I thought all Christians believed the same thing. However, I quickly learned that's not always the case.

As a fresh believer I became planted in an independent Baptist Church. I was very passionate about God, and I was determined to share Jesus with others. Right from day one my heart's desire was for others to experience the same miracle working power that had set me free.

I would often read the book of Acts and would relate to the countless stories of God healing the sick and delivering people from demons— that's exactly what He did for me! I knew that God was calling me to work with Him in the same way as the disciples of the New Testament. I knew that God still wants to see multitudes healed, delivered and saved. But when I began to express these thoughts to my Bible study group in this Baptist Church, I was met with strong resistance. It was then that I realised that not all Christians believe the same way. In fact, this particular Church was *Cessationist*.

What Do Cessationists Believe?

In simple terms, Cessationists believe that the gifts of the Spirit as taught in 1 Corinthians 12, 13 and 14, the ascension ministry offices as taught in Ephesians 4:11, along with all the amazing miracles of the New Testament; have ceased. This is not to say that they believe God cannot heal or perform a miracle today as a rare, sovereign act; they maintain that He is God and can do whatever He wants. However, Cessationists teach that modern believers do not have the same authority or empowerment to heal the sick or perform miracles as the disciples of the New Testament. In other words, they believe that the dynamite power and supernatural gifts died out with the Apostles. They believe the purpose of the gifts of the Spirit was to only validate the gospel and establish the early Church. Now that the Church has the completed canonised scriptures in the sixty-six books of the Bible, Cessationists teach that there is no longer a need for miracles, gifts of the Holy Spirit, or the five-fold ministry offices.

It was an interesting time for me in this Baptist cessationist Church. I had just come out of this radical encounter with the Holy Spirit where I was delivered from demonic spirits, alcoholism and drug addiction. I knew it was the dunamis, miracle-working power that destroyed the works of the devil in my life! Yet I found myself in this Cessationist home-group where they challenged me on the ministry of the Holy Spirit. They were incredible people and I was learning many valuable things from them, but I knew that their teaching on the gifts of the Spirit having passed away was totally incorrect.

My heart's desire was to go to the streets, to preach the gospel, pray for the sick, and do what the disciples of the New Testament had done. To do what I saw the Bible telling me to do. However, my Cessationist friends would tell me that Christians don't do that anymore. They would say we are to "Preach the Roman's road." They were all for preaching the gospel, but they would say healing and the gifts of the Spirit no longer have a place in Christianity. Sadly, they would even go as far as saying that Christians claiming to move in miracles were operating in false signs and wonders.

Original Gospel, Original Results

During this time my Bible study group leader was also a school Teacher. She worked with a lady who had just seen her

son get radically saved, healed and delivered. My Bible study Teacher heard about his testimony and thought it would be a great idea to invite him to our study group to share his story. I'm so extremely thankful that she did because that young man is now my best friend and leader of the movement
'*Awakening*'— his name is Ben Fitzgerald.

At this stage Ben was a new Christian, only a few years old in the Lord. He came along to our Bible study and shared on the miracle-working power of God. It was such a blessing to me as we had very similar testimonies. I knew this was a divine appointment from God.

Ben and I became best friends after that day; it was just what I needed! Ben and I started hitting the streets together almost every day. This is really where I learned how to minister to others. Ben had carried radical faith from very early on in his walk with Jesus. He began to show me how to cast out devils and heal the sick. Man, we saw the craziest miracles! Even today I think back to those times and marvel at what God did through two young men who were just newly saved.

I remember a time when Ben and I were hitting the streets every day preaching the Gospel, praying for the sick and seeing miracles flow. We weren't in full time ministry yet; we were just two young guys asking God to be His vessels. We were hungry for Him to use us in a mighty way to bring Him glory!

There was a city in Victoria, Australia, called Frankston that had a notorious reputation. We would walk the streets of Frankston looking for opportunities to ignite the dynamite.

One day, Ben and I were hanging around outside a shopping centre when we noticed a guy walking in our direction. His face was all bloodied, he looked as though he had been in a punch-up. We thought he was the perfect candidate to hear the gospel!

We ran up to him and began telling him about how much Jesus loves and cares for him. But he was quite distressed and wasn't interested in hearing anything about Jesus; as it turned out, he had just been mugged! His wallet, along with all his rent that he had just collected together to pay his landlord, had been stolen. I sensed God's encouragement and so I knew Ben and I were to press in. I kept asking him to let us pray for him, but he kept refusing. Eventually I said, "C'mon man, you got nothing to lose. Let us pray".

And then Ben boldly declared, "Let us pray for you and God will get your money back".

When Ben said this I had a thought that maybe God wanted me to gift this man some cash. While Ben continued to chat with him, I snuck away to the ATM to withdraw some money. However, I had forgotten that I had already made a large withdrawal from my bank account earlier that day and my account had a daily withdrawal limit. I wasn't able to withdraw a single note to gift the man!

I returned to Ben and the man, and he finally decided to let Ben and I pray for him. We began seeking God and asking Him to somehow return the stolen amount to our new friend.

Suddenly as we were praying, we felt a great rush of wind blow around us. This was really weird because it wasn't a windy day at all and the way the shops are positioned in this outdoor area would normally break the wind. But this wind was so strong that all of us opened our eyes. As we did, we saw two crisp notes, $50 and a $10 note falling like maple leaves right in front of our eyes! I believe that angels were ministering in that moment to back our prayer up with signs and wonders. We all began to jump with joy that God would do something so incredibly wild, like, make money appear out of thin air. But then I wondered, why did only $60 appear when the guy's rent was more than that? So, we prayed again.

This time within 30 seconds of praying for complete provision, the man's phone rings. It was his Dad whom he hadn't spoken to in two years calling him in that very moment! His Dad said, "Son, I just felt to call and ask if everything's OK?"

The guy told his father everything that had just happened. How he was mugged, that his rent money was stolen, that he ran into two guys guys who wanted to pray for him, and how God answered their prayers by making $60 appear in the air. The man's father was so moved by the story that he decided to give his son the rest of the money to make up the difference needed to pay his rent!

To me, this was an even more powerful miracle than money appearing. In that moment God had just healed the fractured relationship between this father and son. Their relationship had been severed for two years and was now being healed and restored by Jesus! This guy was blown away by the power of prayer. When we first met him, he was an atheist, after the money appeared he was agnostic, and with the restoring of his relationship with his father he was ready to receive Jesus as his Lord and Saviour! So, we prayed one more time, this time to see the ultimate miracle of his relationship being restored with his Heavenly Father. We led him in the sinner's prayer and that day he was born again!

You need to understand that wild things such as this were happening frequently on the streets. I was so excited by what God was doing that I wanted to share what was happening with my leaders in the cessationist Baptist Church. Demons were being cast out, money was supernaturally appearing after prayer, and dramatic healings! These were not a one-off sovereign acts; this was happening consistently. We were experiencing notable miracles that could not be denied. I even started bringing people I had led to Jesus on the streets to the Bible studies. Still being quite naive, I expected my study group and leaders to be just as excited as I was. Unfortunately, I was met with a very different response and later in this chapter I'll share what I faced.

Addressing Cessationism

As I mentioned earlier, Cessationists believe miracles have passed away because the Church now has the perfect scriptures. I too believe the canon scriptures are perfect. In fact, that's why I believe the way that I do! It is the Bible that *instructs* me to pursue the supernatural! The Bible instructs me to go into all the world and lay hands on the sick! (Mark 16:18) The Bible tells me that these supernatural signs will follow those who believe!

(Mark 16:17). The scriptures tell me that Jesus said, *"he who believes in Me, the works that I do he will do also; and greater works than these he will do"* (John 14:12). The Bible teaches me that Apostles, Prophets, Evangelists, Pastors, and Teachers are still needed today. Why? Because the role of these five-fold offices didn't cease when the Bible came into its full completed form, but it continues *"till we all come to the unity of the faith and of the knowledge of the Son of God, to a perfect man, to the measure of the stature of the fullness of Christ;"* (Ephesians 4:13).

After being confronted with these incorrect doctrines by the leaders in this Baptist Church I began to really study the scriptures. I searched through the Bible looking for where it says that miracles have ceased. You know what I found? It's not in there! Nowhere in the Bible does it teach that the gifts of the Spirit and the five-fold ministers have ceased, nor that miracle-working power has come to an end. After fervently studying the scriptures on this subject, I challenged my leaders in a loving way with what I had found. I told them I couldn't find any scriptures in the Bible to support their teaching. So, they pointed to two passages that seemingly supported their Cessationist doctrine: 1 Corinthians 13:8-13 and Hebrews 1:1-2. But upon studying the two passages myself, I quickly discovered that they had been taken out of context. Let me share with you what Holy Spirit revealed to me when I searched out these scriptures in their true context.

That Which Is Perfect Has Come

In 1 Corinthians 13:8-13 it says:

> *Love never fails. But whether there are prophecies, they will fail; whether there are tongues, they will cease; whether there is knowledge, it will vanish away.* **For we know in part and we prophesy in part. But when that which is perfect has come, then that which is in part will be done away.** *When I was a child, I spoke as a child, I understood as a child, I thought as a child; but when I became a man, I put away childish things. For now we see in a mirror, dimly, but then face to face. Now I know in part, but then I shall know just as I also am known. And now abide faith, hope, love, these three; but the greatest of these is love.* (Emphasis added).

Cessationists point to this passage of scripture and use it to argue that the gifts of the Spirit are finished. They believe that the statement *"That which is perfect has come"*, is referring to the canon scriptures. However, this is a very poor interpretation of scripture. The statement *"That which is perfect has come"* is in reference to when we come *"face-to-face"* with Jesus in eternity! In other words, the gifts of the Spirit will cease once we are in Heaven, when we are absent from the body and present with the Lord (2 Corinthians 5:8). Then, we'll be face-to-face with Jesus, not with the written pages on this Earth, but actually face-to-face with Jesus in Heaven! And in Heaven, we're not going to speak in tongues, we're not going to need to prophesy, and we won't need to do any miracles to confirm the gospel because everyone in Heaven will already be saved! The rescue mission will be complete and there will be no more death, sorrow, or crying! (Revelation 21:4).

We need the miracle-working power *now!* While on the Earth in our fallen state, we absolutely still need the gifts of the Spirit. The Church is the hands and feet of Jesus! We partner with Him to bring forth God's Kingdom through our earthly vessels. If the Church needed miracle-working power in the days of the Bible, then we absolutely need it today! Because the devil's time is short and he's causing more destruction now than ever before. So, we see very clearly through scripture that the gifts have not passed away.

This was when I started to really understand the importance of correct hermeneutics — the principles of interpretation. Such as systematic theology, knowing what the whole Bible says on a matter. And studying passages in their entire and correct context.

God Has Spoken

The second passage Cessationist leaders pointed to in an attempt to support their beliefs was Hebrews 1:1-2:

> *God, who at various times and in various ways spoke in time past to the fathers by the prophets, 2 has in these last days* **spoken to us by His S***on, whom He has appointed heir of all things, through whom also He made the worlds;* (emphasis added).

Cessationists point to this scripture to argue that God doesn't speak prophetically through people today because *"in these last days spoken to us by His Son"*. They teach that in modern times God exclusively speaks through the canon scriptures. In other words, now that we have the completed Bible there is no need for Prophets or Apostles. However, that's not what the author of Hebrews is communicating at all. We need to take a closer look at Hebrews 1:1-2 and rightly determine what this passage is, and isn't, saying.

Jesus Christ Is Supreme Revelation

In the Old Testament, God spoke to humanity at different times and in different ways. For example, God spoke to Moses, Joshua, the Prophets, and the Priests. But in these last days God has spoken through His Son.

I believe what the Bible is saying is clear; in comparison to speaking through Old Testament figures such as Moses and the Prophets, Jesus Christ is the supreme revelation. What do I mean by that? The Bible describes Jesus as being the express image, or perfect example and representation, of the Father (Hebrews 1:3). That's what Hebrews 1 is saying. The revelation through Jesus is superior to any other revelation. He's the perfect and complete message of God; He's the ultimate understanding of God. God revealed Himself in various ways in the past (Hebrews 1:1) but Jesus is now the perfect representation of God the father. He

Himself said He was the fulfilment of the Old Testament law and the Old Testament revelation (Matthew 5:17).

Those who have the Son have the Father, but those who reject the Son, reject the Father (Matthew 10:40, 1 John 2:23). If you reject the supreme revelation, then you reject the Father. Jesus is higher than all the angels (Hebrews 1:4), His name is above all names (Philippians 2:9), and He's the pioneer and captain of our salvation (Hebrews 2:10). In a nutshell, *that's* what Hebrews 1:1-2 is saying. Now, let's look at what it isn't saying.

God Speaks Today

The author of Hebrews is not saying that God no longer speaks through the Holy Spirit or prophecy. This passage is not saying that God only speaks through the canon scriptures. The Bible doesn't say that and Hebrews 1:1-2 certainly isn't saying that either.

It's clear, that through Pentecost to the second coming, God is still speaking through the gift of prophecy. He is not exclusively speaking through the logos (the cannon scriptures) — although, we can agree that there is no more sure word than the written Word of God (2 Peter 1:19). But that doesn't mean we should take it a step further and say God is exclusively speaking through the Bible. To believe that is a great error, and you won't find it anywhere in the scriptures. That's why I'm passionate about giving an answer for why it is that we believe what we believe. We aren't shying away from solid theology, we want to give a Biblical answer to the harsh, religious critics and this sort of teaching.

John 15:26 says, *"But when the Helper comes, whom I shall send to you from the Father, the Spirit of truth who proceeds from the Father, He will testify of Me"*. The Son is still speaking to us today, not only through canon scripture, but through the Holy Spirit. John 16:8 says, *"And when He has come, He will convict the world of sin, and of righteousness, and of judgment"*.

You would notice that the above passage doesn't say, *"When the canon scriptures come it will guide you through all truth"*. The canon scriptures certainly do guide us and God does speak to us through them, but in these above verses Jesus is encouraging us that the Spirit of truth will speak to us and guide us also. The Spirit of truth speaks on the behalf of Jesus, taking what is His and declaring it to us (John 16:13-15). I want to give you another scriptural example of how the Holy Spirit can speak and lead us today. Acts 16:6-7 says:

> *Now when they had gone through Phrygia and the region of Galatia,* **they were forbidden by the Holy Spirit to preach the word in Asia**. *After they had come to Mysia, they tried to go into Bithynia, but the Spirit did not permit them.*

It wasn't the canon scriptures that had forbidden Paul and his team from preaching in Asia, it was the Holy Spirit who spoke to them. And once they had come to Mysia and tried to go to Bithynia, once again they weren't stopped by the scriptures; it was the Holy Spirit who *"did not permit them"*. It was Jesus speaking through the Spirit of truth that did not allow them to continue to Bithynia.

It is the same way today, Jesus doesn't only speak through the scriptures but through His Holy Spirit, and we can see that very much alive and active in the New Testament.

The Open Cannon

Some Cessationists like my old Baptist leaders would probably try to argue at this point that my examples were of events that took place during a time period we call the '*open cannon'*, meaning the cannon scripture were not yet established. However, this is a weak argument because the Bible itself doesn't say that the Holy Spirit will stop speaking to us once the cannon scriptures have been put together.

In the gospel of Mark, Jesus gave us some insight into today's times before His return. Mark 13:9-11 says:

> *"But watch out for yourselves, for they will deliver you up to councils, and you will be beaten in the synagogues. You will be brought before rulers and kings for My sake, for a testimony to them. And the gospel must first be preached to all the nations. But when they arrest you and deliver you up, do not worry beforehand, or premeditate what you will speak.* ***But whatever is given you in that hour, speak that; for it is not you who speak, but the Holy Spirit.*** (Emphasis added).

Hopefully any scholar would agree that these words refer to a time after which the cannon is closed. At this point in the world's timeline, you probably won't be allowed to have a Bible in your hand. But you will have the Holy Spirit! You see, God speaks through His Holy Spirit and through His people! Through the power of the Holy Spirit, and prophetic gift we don't need to fear what to say in that hour because God will give us the words! He will speak through us as His body and as His ambassador.

The Holy Spirit is indeed still speaking and always will; from Pentecost right through to His second coming. Until we are all in Heaven we need that gift of prophecy through the Holy Spirit.

That was the final Scripture point to debunk. Hebrews 1:1-2 is not teaching that God only speaks through the canon scriptures today. We have examined what Hebrews 1:1-2 is saying as well as what it certainly isn't saying. And that's systematic theology; it lines up with Genesis through to Revelation. It lines up with the perfect canon scriptures. We can be sure that God is still speaking prophetically to the Church today. There are still apostles needed today, there are still Prophets needed today, and the gifts of the Spirit are still active today. In fact, I'd say they are more necessary in these end times than ever before.

Dr Michael Brown hits the nail on the head when he said:

If Hebrews 1:1-2 teaches that, since God's final revelation came through His Son, the gift of prophecy has ceased, then why did it continue throughout NT times, as well as *for centuries after? That's obviously not the implication of God's final revelation coming through the Son.*9

Sadly, many in the Baptist home group remained hardhearted towards the miracle dynamite power of God. Eventually God led me out of that group and into another Church. I didn't allow myself to be offended by them and I'm grateful for that season during which God allowed me to be exposed to different types of teaching. I believe I wouldn't be the man I am today without such experiences.

Finally, I want to encourage believers to never be intimidated by religious people. It was the Pharisees and the Sadducees, which were the religious people of the day, who opposed the miracle dynamite power of God. In fact, they went as far as accusing Jesus of operating by the power of Beelzebub, rather than the power of God (Luke 11:15). But Jesus didn't allow Himself to be distracted; He continued to press on with His mission, igniting the dynamite and destroying the works of the devil.

CHARACTER BEFORE ANOINTING

Moving in miracle-working power should go hand-in-hand with witnessing to people about Jesus. Still, we don't want to teach on power without emphasising the importance of character and godly living. We want to run the race and finish well as faithful sons and daughters. We don't want to focus on power at the cost of knowing Him and living a godly life. Power is vital to the Christian walk, but it should be accessed relationally with God. We want to hear His voice, know His heart, and be marked by His presence. As believers, when we love God and cast our daily affection upon Him, we can't help hearing His heartbeat for the lost and broken. It is from this place of intimacy with the Father that our desire to ignite the dynamite should be sparked. In this chapter, we're going to unpack what it looks like to move in power with the right motives and to live a life of holiness.

Compassion In Action

We see in the scriptures that Jesus was moved with compassion, I believe this was partly because of His intimate relationship with the Father. He would often get away from the crowds to be alone with the Father on the mountain. The gospels record on multiple occasions that Jesus said, *"The Son can do nothing of Himself, but what He sees the Father do"* (John 5:19). I believe this was because Jesus spent time with the Father. He was intimate with God, He heard the Father's voice, and He responded to the Father's heartbeat for people. He was fully man and fully God, but He needed to spend time with the Father in an intimate relationship to flow and move according to His Father's will. And of course, we know it's the Father's will that none should perish (2 Peter 3:9) and that all would be healed (1 Peter 2:24, Psalm 103:1-3).

We read in the Bible that Jesus was moved with compassion (Matthew 14:14). That means the Father's will to see none perish and for all to be healed comes from a place of loving compassion. The motive to see the dynamite ignited is His love for people. Godly motives are essential in the Christian walk. Jesus was moved with compassion; He was motivated by love. He wasn't driven by fame, or about how many 'likes' He received on Facebook or Instagram. His heart was aligned with the Father's.

I think as believers, we need to remember that's why we do what we do. It's part of the simple, royal commandment to love God and to love people. And if you feel as though you lack compassion, I encourage you to seek God in the secret place. Get alone with Him, find your mountain-top, and you will rediscover the heartbeat of Heaven.

The gospel of Matthew tells us of the time when the religious leaders of the day questioned Jesus, asking Him, what is the greatest commandment? And Jesus responded:

> ***You shall love the Lord your God with all your heart, with all your soul, and with all your mind.'*** *This is the first and great commandment. And the second is like it:* ***'You shall love your neighbor as yourself.'*** *On these two commandments hang all the Law and the Prophets.* (Matthew 22:37-40, emphasis added).

If we really love our neighbour, we're going to want to see the works of the devil destroyed in their lives. We're going to want to know how to ignite that dynamite. If we really love people, then we will earnestly desire the spiritual gifts (1 Corinthians 14:1); we will hunger and thirst for God's power to flow through us so that people can be set free.

The Importance Of Godly Character

If Jesus, being fully man and yet fully God, needed to spend time with the Father then how much more do we? If we don't spend time with the Father, in our humanity we can fall into selfish ambition or the wrong motives in our ministry. If we're not abiding in prayer we can easily fall into temptation and the deceitfulness of sin. Jesus teaches this when in the garden of Gethsemane, He says to his disciples, *"Watch and pray, lest you enter into temptation. The Spirit is willing, but the flesh is weak."* (Matthew 26:41).

Our character and our relationship with the Father is foundational to igniting the dynamite. Character in itself is a witness and can often speak volumes without saying a thing.

My heart for this chapter is that I not only teach on miracle-working power, but to emphasise the importance of character and godly living. In Matthew 7:21-23, Jesus said:

> *'Not everyone who says to Me, 'Lord, Lord,' shall enter the kingdom of heaven, but he who does the will of My Father in heaven. Many will say to Me in that day, 'Lord, Lord, have we not prophesied in Your name, cast out demons in Your name, and done many wonders in Your name?'* ***And***

then I will declare to them, 'I never knew you; depart from Me, you who practice lawlessness!' (Emphasis added).

I believe the people Jesus is referring to literally did cast out devils, they did prophesy, and they did perform wonders in the name of Jesus. I believe they were operating in the dynamite power and the gifts of the Spirit. And yet, we see Jesus reject them even though they were operating in the supernatural. I believe the reason is clear, "*I never knew you, depart from Me, you who practise lawlessness.*" The word **practise** is the keyword here. Jesus isn't talking about weak Christians; He's talking about habitual, unrepentant sin. People who don't really know God, although they claim to, however they don't know Him or they have turned away from Him.

The Deceitfulness Of Habitual Sin

It is also possible that the people referred to in Matthew 7:21-23, did know God and were genuinely born-again to start with. They could have been genuinely baptised in the Holy Spirit and had begun their race very well but later fallen prey to seducing spirits. The Bible says, *"in latter times some will depart from the faith, giving heed to seducing spirits and doctrines of demons"* (1 Timothy 4:1). It is likely that these types of people are seduced by deceiving spirits and are led back into habitual sinful practises.

For example, a Pastor starts really well, operating in the prophetic, signs and wonders, and leading a great movement. Then, all-of-a-sudden, things go wrong, and he has an affair. He falls into sinful practises such as adultery, or other sexual sins. At the same time, he remains in active ministry while still living in unrepentant sin. He, therefore, deceives himself into thinking that he hasn't lost God's approval over his life because miracles are still present in his ministry.

The Trap of Deception

I once knew a minister whom I believe loved God and was genuinely flowing in the prophetic. At first, he bore the fruit of a Christian. However, because of pressure to perform and wanting to have a greater level of accuracy, after some time he fell into the temptation of looking on Facebook before his meetings to attain information so as to fabricate Words of Knowledge. He would check the event page to see who had clicked going and then he would search a few profiles to attain certain information about them, such as their occupation, any addresses, or even the names of their family. He would appear to receive incredibly accurate information from the Holy Spirit but then prophesy general stuff. It looked like Holy Spirit on the surface, but really it was social media. This man did this for months, and even years, with no one questioning him. This sort of minister is what we call a 'Google Prophet.'

One day this man came to minister at our Church, and we sensed that something was off. So, we confronted him. To his credit this particular guy took the correction to heart and repented. I won't say any names but he genuinely repented. He stepped down from his immediate ministry, he went through the process of being corrected and accountable to others, and he realigned his character and got his life right with God. We really celebrate his willingness to accept correction and take the time to develop good character, because there was the potential for real damage to be done to the body of Christ.

This sort of false practise has been going on for a long time. I heard of another couple back in the '70s who would conspire together to create false Words of Knowledge. When the people arrived at their meetings they were given specific information cards to fill out. People would fill out the cards with their personal information and their prayer needs. While the man would minister from the stage, his wife would read the information cards. She would use an earpiece to communicate to him various personal details written on the cards. The man would then use the information to fabricate Words of Knowledge.

That kind of counterfeit causes people to doubt the genuine. Releasing false Words of Knowledge can damage the genuine move of the prophetic. It is so important that we don't get our identity from gifting. If we do then there's pressure to perform. If our identity relies on our gifting, then we're only as good as our next Word of Knowledge, or our next prophetic word. Our identity must rest on whom God is and what He says and thinks of us.

The Bible says to take heed lest you fall (1 Corinthians 10:12). We take these examples as a warning. Our heart is that we all learn from these sad stories and remain in a place of humility; to encourage you to remain in the wisdom of the Lord and to remain close to Him. We need to stay in His ways, so that we don't fall prey to the wiles of the enemy.

Biblical-Grace vs Hyper-Grace

Some people may question Jesus when He says, "*I never knew you*". They can think: *How could God have never known them? How then did they operate in the supernatural?* It's important when studying the Bible that we apply correct hermeneutics and that we allow scripture to interpret scripture because that's how we develop accurate doctrine. I think Ezekiel 18:24 gives us great insight into what's happening in the Matthew 7 passage when it says:

> ***But when a righteous man turns away from his righteousness and commits iniquity, and does according to all the abominations that the wicked man does, shall he live?*** *All the righteousness which he has done* ***shall not be remembered; because of the unfaithfulness of which he is guilty and the sin which he has committed****, because of them he shall die.* (Emphasis added).

If someone turns from their right-standing with God and returns to a life of unrepentant iniquity, God will not remember their past righteousness. This is the balance of biblical grace VS hyper-grace. The good news is when we repent and turn to God and His righteousness, the Bible says He forgets our iniquity (Hebrews 8:12). As far as the East is from the West, He has removed our transgressions from us (Psalm 103:12). However, in the same way, if we turn away from God and return to the practise of iniquity, God will not remember us nor the previous good works that we did.

The Gifts Are Irrevocable

People have often asked me over the years: *How is it possible for someone to move in signs and wonders and yet be involved in some form of habitual sinful practise?*

In Romans 11:29 it says, *"For the gifts and calling of God are irrevocable."* The KJV describes them as being *"without repentance."* This means, believers can be operating in their gifting or calling and moving in power, yet sadly, still be in habitual sin. If they continue without repentance, they will eventually grieve the Holy Spirit out of the recesses of their heart and begin to operate out of a counterfeit spirit. That's when it becomes false signs and wonders.

We could be an anointed preacher, and we could be mighty in the scriptures like Apollos, we could move in signs, wonders, and the anointing; and yet in our personal life we could be in habitual sin. Or in our day-to-day life, such as in our workplace or home-life we could be stealing money or addicted to pornography. And so our character falls. This can be really damaging for the people we're trying to reach with the Gospel, and it could also have devastating effects on our own eternal salvation.

However, on the other side of the coin, if our character is in the right place, if we're humble, teachable, honest, and are demonstrating the fruit of the Spirit in terms of our character; that in itself is a witness and speaks a thousand words. Jesus said, *"by their fruits you will know them"* (Matthew 7:20).

You Will Know Them By Their Fruit

We know that an orange tree is an orange tree because it produces oranges. We know an apple tree is an apple tree because it produces apples. Normally we don't discern an apple tree by the root system, nor by the trunk, but we recognise the tree by the fruit it bears. In the same way, if professing Christians are producing habitual sin in their lives, then we need to question whether they are genuinely Christian. But if they are producing the fruit of the Spirit in their lives, then that is the evidence of a genuine born-again heart. *"The fear of the lord is the beginning of wisdom"* (Proverbs 9:10). My prayer is that this chapter will cause you to have a healthy fear of God. We're in awe of God, but we fear turning our back on Him and returning to a place of habitual sin. Even though we see miracles and operate in the supernatural, we don't ever want to enter into lawlessness and the deceitfulness of sin.

Weak vs Wicked

There is a difference between *weak* and *wicked*. So, the passage where Jesus says, *"I never knew you, depart from me, you who **practise** lawlessness,"* the word practise refers to continual unrepentant sin. That would come into the category of *wicked*. When people think they can continue in sexual immorality or continue in habitual sin and still minister in the name of Jesus; that's wicked.

There is a difference when we have a weak moment and make a mistake but are repentant. 1 John 2:1 says, *"My little children, these things I write to you, so that you may not sin. And if anyone sins, we have an Advocate with the Father, Jesus Christ the righteous."* It says *if anyone sins.* It doesn't say *when you sin.* It says *if anyone sins.* So, it shouldn't be a normal thing for a Christian to sin. It says if we sin, we have an advocate; we have Jesus who stands on our behalf and He cleanses us from our sin. There's a difference between weak and wicked. We need to be careful because it's possible to fall into a place of practising lawlessness and being wicked while still performing signs and wonders.

If you have an area of weakness or you've had a bad day or a bad week, I want to encourage you to not fall into a place of condemnation, thinking that God's power can't flow through you anymore. Just because you've had a bad day, or you're feeling weak, doesn't mean His power leaves you, or that you've lost your salvation. The Bible says the anointing abides (1 John 2:27), it doesn't come and go depending on whether you're having a bad day or not.

The Bible calls for us to be holy as He is holy (1 Peter 1:16). So, of course, we want to champion people to walk in holiness and right character. However, if you do have a bad day, don't fall into a place of doubt, thinking that the power can no longer operate through you. We need a balance. Both 'Hyper-grace' and

'Hyper-holiness' are dangerous. We want to warn people from wickedness, but we don't want them to feel condemned if they're weak in an area. There's no condemnation for those in Christ Jesus, who don't walk according to the flesh but according to the Spirit (Romans 8:1). We don't walk or practise the fleshly deeds, but we do walk in the Spirit. If we stumble in sin, we confess and repent. We have Jesus as our incredible advocate who cleanses us from sin. We brush ourselves off, and we thank God that there's no condemnation. We stay in that place of faith, knowing that the anointing abides in and for believers. We remain in faith, believing that the sick can still be healed even if we're having a bad day.

And finally, when we have a weak moment or stumble in the flesh, that doesn't change who we are. This is why knowing our identity in Christ is so important. The Bible says that when we become born-again and are spirit-filled, we are made righteous. It's not according to our own righteousness; He has given us *His* righteousness (2 Corinthians 5:21). The Bible says we once had a sinful nature (Romans 6:6), but now through Christ Jesus and the finished work of the cross, we are partakers of His divine nature (2 Peter 1:4).

SIGNS AND WONDERS WITH THE TRUTH

In our pursuit to ignite the dynamite let's never forget the main thing which is seeing people saved through the preaching of the gospel.

Operating in signs and wonders is a way to help lead people to Jesus. Miracles are signs that make people wonder, and it's a sign that points people to the way. It's sowing a seed that helps lead them into salvation. The apostle Paul said in the Bible, "*I planted, Apollos watered, but God gave the increase*" (1 Corinthians 3:6). Ultimately, God is the one who saves souls.

Sharing The Full Counsel Of God

We don't want to demonstrate the supernatural power of God and see people healed, only to neglect sharing with them the life-giving message of the full Gospel. It is the Gospel that is the power of God for salvation (Romans 1:16). Signs and wonders will follow the preaching of the Gospel; indeed, they should support the preaching of the Gospel. God does want to heal people, but it would be incredibly sad if their body is healed, yet they were still on their way to hell.

In John 5:14, Jesus healed a man on the Sabbath and this caused a stir among the religious leaders. After Jesus healed the man, He withdrew from the crowd. This is more than likely because He knew that the religious leaders would persecute Him for healing on the Sabbath. Later, Jesus found the man He had healed in the temple and said to him, *"See you have been made well, sin no more, lest a worst thing come upon you"* (John 5:14). Jesus didn't just heal the man's body; He gave him the truth that would set his soul free (John 8:32). The truth is we are not to continue in sin; we need to repent from sin and yield our life to God. This is a crucial part of the gospel that must be proclaimed.

We cannot rely on miracles alone to lead people to Jesus; we cannot be afraid to tell them the truth. Sometimes miracles will cause people to fall to their knees and give their lives to Him, but sometimes it won't.

The Bible says Jesus is full of grace *and* truth (John 1:14). As Christians, we need to be careful that we don't see Jesus only through the lens of grace and forget about the necessity of truth. On the other hand, sometimes we only view Jesus through the lens of truth and forget His grace. Mature Christians understand the necessity for both grace and truth.

They understand that Jesus is both the lion and the lamb.

There were times when Jesus would rebuke entire cities. Jesus said:

> ***Woe to you, Chorazin! Woe to you, Bethsaida!*** *For if the mighty works which were done in you had been done in Tyre and Sidon, they would have repented long ago, sitting in sackcloth and ashes"* (Luke 10:13, emphasis added).

Jesus released His grace and goodness through many signs and wonders in these cities, but it didn't lead them to repentance. This grieved His heart because He loved them. Jesus didn't desire to see these cities perish, but He loved them enough to speak the truth to them and warn them of the destruction to come.

Miracles alone won't save someone. The truth of the gospel is the power of God unto salvation (Romans 1:16). We celebrate the miracles, and we celebrate the signs and wonders, but we cannot omit the saving truth of the gospel.

Let me share a story with you of how signs and wonders helped a man who was searching to find the absolute truth of Jesus.

Some years ago, my wife and I planted our first Church in Queensland. A guy named Donovan started coming to our meetings to check them out. After one Sunday service, I was discussing with Donovan and learned that he had been invited to Church by one of our street-team members. Donovan told me about his journey to try to discover the truth. The problem was, he was searching in all the wrong places. He had been to the Freemasons, the Buddhist temple, the Hindu temple, the Mormons, and had tried a whole list of other false spiritual paths. He was a nice guy, and I could tell he was genuine in his search, but he said he wasn't convinced that he had found the truth.

At this particular service, I was teaching on miracles and sharing testimonies from our street-teams of God healing and performing signs and wonders. Donovan was intrigued; he hadn't heard of the miraculous from any of the other faiths he had visited.

Later that week, I was leading a home-group in a Bible study when suddenly I received a call from a distressed Donovan. His best-mate had just been mowed down by a bus and rushed to the Intensive Care Unit at the Royal Brisbane Hospital. He feared for his friend's life and in his desperation to find help, he didn't call the Freemasons, he didn't call the Buddhist or Hindu temple— He called us. He called the Christians. He called the right people because Jesus is the one who heals and delivers! Jesus is the way, the truth, and the life (John 14:6).

At that moment I felt the Holy Spirit urging me to go with Donovan to the hospital. The home-group went into a time of prayer and intercession for the friend as I rushed to the hospital.

When Donovan and I arrived at the hospital, we learned that his friend's injuries were severe. As well as the cuts, swelling and bruising that covered his body, he had a lacerated liver and a perforated lung. He was in a horrific situation.

I received permission to pray for him in his hospital room. I laid my hands on him and said a simple prayer. To be honest, I didn't feel anything. Sometimes when we pray for people, we feel something; we can feel the presence of the Holy Spirit fill the room. But on this occasion, I didn't feel anything. I just prayed by faith, without fear of what his family or anyone else was thinking of me. I just believed and decreed the Word over him. I would have only been with him for about ten minutes.

The next day I heard from an excited Donovan. During the night, he slept in his friend's hospital room to keep him company. With his very own eyes he watched as every single bruise visibly vanished! By morning, all of his friend's bruising was gone!

Within three days he was fully healed, including the serious injuries to his vital organs!

Donovan had witnessed a miracle. In the midst of his searching for truth, in the midst of him exploring other religions and spiritual practises, he called a Christian for help. Why? Because when he went to Church on Sunday, he heard that our God heals. His mate's miraculous recovery was a sign and wonder that led Donovan to Jesus! It was the power of God that opened Donovan's heart to repentance and paved the way for me to share the full gospel of God with him. The miracle opened his heart to receive the truth he was looking for. I said to him, *"You've got to repent from sin, you've got to turn your life from darkness. There's no other God. You can't follow after false gods, or false spirits and practises."*

I shared with him the full truth found in Jesus Christ, and he joyfully accepted Jesus Christ into his life as Lord and Saviour. He went on to be plugged into the local Church and ended up leading many people to Jesus himself.

Preaching truth, whether it be declaring Jesus as the only way or the necessity to turn from sin, is essential. Jesus said, *"And you shall know the truth, and the truth shall make you free"* (John 8:32).

A Man-Saving Gospel, Not A False Man-Pleasing Gospel

I believe, sometimes we avoid hard truth because we want to be liked by everyone. It's man-pleasing before God-pleasing, and really, that comes down to the fear of man.

Don't get me wrong; we don't want to be obnoxious. It's good to be graceful and loving, and it's good when people are pleased with us. However, we need to understand that, as Christians, we are not going to be liked by everyone. In fact, sometimes you'll be hated, just like how Jesus was hated. Following Jesus means we will be persecuted, Jesus said, *"If the world hates you, you know that it hated Me before it hated you"* (John 15:18). As Christians we love to talk about the precious promises of God in scripture. We love the promises of healing, deliverance, and freedom as we should because those are incredible promises that are core to our faith. Sometimes, however, we forget the promise of persecution. We forget that Jesus said, *"If they persecuted Me, they will also persecute you"* (John 15:20). It is because of this hard truth that the world hates us and persecutes us.

I believe that's why sometimes we shy away from preaching the whole gospel and the truth of the Bible on certain matters. If we fear man over God, we become afraid of being hated by the world and alter the message to become more man-pleasing. This is a serious and dangerous thing to do. The apostle Paul severely warned the Church against perverting the true gospel, saying, *"if anyone preaches any other gospel to you than what you have received, let him be accursed"* (Galatians 1:9). When we pervert the gospel to please men, we are not only hindering others from being set free, but we are placing ourselves under a curse. When we please men over God, we move from serving Christ to serving men. Paul goes on to say, *"For do I now persuade men, or God? Or do I seek to please men? For if I still pleased men, I would not be a bondservant of Christ"* (Galatians 1:10).

The Word of God is described as being like a sword (Hebrews 4:12). Its purpose is not to tickle ears but instead to pierce hearts. It brings conviction and change. So don't water it down, preach God's truth! The Bible says, *"And you shall know the truth, and the truth shall make you free"* (John 8:32).

Truth At The Cost Of Followers

John 6 is a great example of the ministry of Jesus and His heart's desire to preach the truth.

The Bible says, *"Then a great multitude followed Him, because they saw His signs which He performed on those who were diseased"* (John 6:2). The crowds followed Jesus because of His signs, and still today it's important for us to understand that signs and wonders will attract crowds. This is not a bad thing, but Jesus wasn't in ministry to entertain the multitudes with miracles. Rather His main mission was to make disciples. To do this He would often preach hard truth (John 6:60). It is the hard truth that exposes the motives of the heart. The Bible says it is the truth of the Word that is *"a discerner of the thoughts and intents of the heart"* (Hebrews 4:12). Some followed Jesus for miracles, others for food (John 6:26). It can be the same today. Only those who follow Jesus because of the truth find everlasting life. Jesus said, *"I am the way, the truth, and the life. No one comes to the Father except through Me"* (John 14:6).

Jesus was willing to preach the truth at the cost of followers. His words were spirit and life (John 6:63), and yet the crowd thought His message was too hard, so they rejected eternal life. Even some of His disciples turned away because they found His words too difficult, *"From that time many of His disciples went back and walked with Him no more"* (John 6:66). It is truly a sad moment when someone will not receive the truth, and therefore they walk away from Jesus.

Jesus even recognised that the twelve apostles were struggling with the hardness of His message, so He asked them, *"Do you also want to go away?"* (John 6:67). Peter's response was amazing! He said, *"Lord, to whom shall we go? You have the words of eternal life"* (John 6:68). For Peter and the apostles, there was no other option. Where could they even go? They may not have understood everything Jesus was saying at that moment, but they knew that Jesus was the Messiah, that He was God, and that He alone had the words of eternal life.

As Christians, sometimes I wonder if we've become afraid of the multitudes walking away from Church, or of losing followers on our Facebook and Instagram pages, and so we avoid the hard truth. Around the time of writing this chapter, my friend Ben Fitzgerald posted a scripture around homosexuality being a sin. He said most of his posts are generally very engaging and he tends to gain followers daily. However, after posting on homosexuality, he lost 500 followers within the hour. Praise God, this loss of followers hasn't changed him. He continues to follow his convictions and to not bow down to the fear of man. But sadly, I believe many ministers shun from preaching the full truth because they fear losing followers.

Today's Hard Truth

What are some of the hard sayings today? There is an immense amount of pressure today against speaking the truth about sin.

One example, as mentioned above, would be the topic of homosexuality. Are we only willing to see the sick healed? Or are we also willing to share the truth that you cannot continue in homosexual practises, or any other sinful practises, and enter into the Kingdom of God?

Another good friend of mine is Pastor Margaret Court, who has repeatedly come under fire for boldly sharing the truth when it comes to human sexuality. Because of her unwavering devotion to the Word of God, she is often excluded and greatly persecuted in the world of tennis. For those who don't know, Margaret Court is the greatest tennis player ever to play the game. She's won more grand slams and tournaments than any other player in history, including Serena Williams, Rod Laver, and Rodger Federer. She should be celebrated like any other world champion, but sadly she's often condemned for simply preaching the Bible. She's a great example of someone that does not shun from preaching the truth, and yet she does it with such grace and love.

What about sexual activity outside of marriage? Sex is a good thing, designed by God for the covenant of marriage. But when you are a single, unmarried person, if your relationship has become sexual, then you need to repent.

We need to ask ourselves, are we willing to be like John the Baptist? John boldly told King Herod that his adulterous relationship was wrong.

Are we also willing to confront sin and preach the repentance side of the Gospel? The Gospel is good news for those who turn away from their sin. When we repent, the Bible says Jesus has, *"delivered us from the power of darkness and hath translated us into the Kingdom of his dear Son"* (Colossians 1:13, KJV). But there needs to be the repentance element with the full counsel of God, and often that is the unpopular aspect of the Gospel.

The reason why we avoid the truth is that we don't want to rock the boat, but Jesus wasn't afraid to rock the boat! He understood that the truth sets people free. We must not shy away from preaching truth and allowing the miracles to be a signpost to Jesus. In conclusion, let's continue to ignite the dynamite, operating in the supernatural power of God by healing the sick and casting out devils; but let's never omit the truth. The miracle working power must always accompany and support the truth of God's Word and the Gospel.

RAISING THE DEAD

In modern Christian culture I have noticed that raising the dead has become more of a fringe subject. This isn't true for everyone; I have some great friends who have seen some incredible miracles, including multiple people raised from the dead. On the whole, I think it is safe to say that in our Western Church culture it is a subject not as commonly taught as healing or leadership.

There could be some fair reasons why it is less spoken of. I know that I haven't had many opportunities to raise the dead. In our Western culture it's different here than it is in countries such as Africa or Mexico. Our medical practices are stricter and are not as lenient in having someone come to pray for a dead person. It's difficult to go to the morgue or to get the ambulance officer's permission to pray for someone who has just died. So, there are fair reasons why we do not see this at the forefront of ministry.

Raising The Dead Is Central

In saying all that, I want to acknowledge that raising the dead is at the very core of our Christian belief. Jesus Christ died on the cross for our sins, but He was also raised from the dead. His death and resurrection are foundational to our salvation. 1 Corinthians 15:17 says, *"And if Christ is not risen, your faith is futile; you are still in your sins!"* That is how foundational it is to our salvation; if we don't believe that Jesus raised from the dead, then our faith is futile, and we're actually still dead in our sins. We shouldn't see raising the dead as a fringe subject, it's actually the core of Christianity!

The miracle of raising the dead is also the one miracle that cannot be counterfeited by the devil. In the Bible, we see the devil counterfeit various miracles. Simon the Sorcerer had such demonic power that the people likened him to a god (Acts 8:9-10). When Moses entered the royal court of Pharaoh, he faced two sorcerers who mocked God by copying the same miracle that God had assigned to Moses and Aaron (Exodus 7:10-12). But there is one miracle the devil cannot counterfeit, and that is raising the dead. Only God can cause a person's spirit to return to their body; only God can create life.

Raising The Dead In Scripture

Raising the dead was not a one-off for Jesus that was limited to His own resurrection. Throughout scripture, there are multiple times where people were raised from the dead. Furthermore, it wasn't only Jesus raising the dead either! Multiple Biblical characters raised the dead through the supernatural power of God.

In the Old Testament, there are multiple accounts of the dead coming back to life. In 1 Kings 17:24, Elijah prayed to God, and life returned to the widow's son. In 2 Kings 4:18-37, Elisha raised the Shunammite's son back to life. In 2 Kings 13:20-21, no one actually prayed for the dead to rise, but a man came back to life after touching the bones of Elisha! I believe this occasion was a sovereign act of God, where there was residual anointing resting on the bones of Elisha that brought back the man's spirit.

The first New Testament account of raising the dead was when Jesus brought back the widow's son in Luke 7:11-17. This was actually the boy's funeral, but Jesus steps in and changes the plan. The son was raised back to life, and Jesus turned what was meant to be a funeral into a praise and worship party. It would have been funny in the days of Jesus, I wonder if the funeral directors were worried about going out of business! I've heard Bill Johnson say, "Jesus ruined every funeral He attended, including His own."

The next New Testament account we read of raising the dead is Jairus's daughter in Luke 8:52-56, and then Lazarus of Bethany in John 11.

Then there's an interesting account of a mass resurrection in Matthew 27:50-53. This happened around the same time of Jesus's own death and resurrection. I believe God caused the graves to open and the dead to come back to life as a sovereign sign and wonder to confirm the death and resurrection of Jesus Christ.

Then, in Acts 9:36, Peter raises Tabitha from the dead. It's interesting to note that the Bible says many believed in God after witnessing this miracle. In fact, we read something similar when Elijah raised the widow's son from the dead. The Bible says that after her son was raised, the widow said to Elijah, *"Now by this I know that you are a man of God, and that the word of the Lord in your mouth is the truth"* (1 Kings 17:24). Raising the dead is a powerful sign that confirms the Gospel or the Word of God.

One of my favourite accounts in the Bible of the dead being raised is found in Acts 20:7-12. The people were hungry to hear the Word of God and Paul was preaching for hours on end. When it came to midnight, a young man named Eutychus became drowsy and fell out of a third-story window and died. Paul wasn't disturbed by the sudden death but instead went down to the boy, embraced him, and prayed him back to life!

When I read this account, I wondered how Paul would have gone preaching in our modern Western culture with our neat little Church services running exactly on time. Can you imagine, with today's modern-day health and safety rules; the whole Church would have gone into panic mode and called the ambulance! It's amazing how nonchalant Paul was about a death in his sermon. He just raised the kid back to life and then went straight back to preaching!

These, of course, are just the dead raising accounts we know of; stories that have been written and recorded in the Bible. But John 21:25 says:

> ***And there are also many other things that Jesus did***, *which if they were written one by one, I suppose that even the world itself could not contain the books that would be written. Amen.* (Emphasis added).

I believe this is true for both the Old Testament and the New Testament; not everything was written down because there wouldn't be enough pages to record the miracles.

There are plenty of Biblical accounts to show that raising the dead is something that God does. I believe it's something we need to press into for today because we want many to believe the Word of God, and we want people to know that what we're saying is not just empty words. Like Paul said, *"And my speech and my preaching were not with persuasive words of human wisdom, but in demonstration of the Spirit and of power"* (1 Corinthians 2:4). There is probably no more powerful miracle, apart from salvation, than raising the dead!

How Should We Pray?

When raising the dead, we see Peter using authority in Christ by commanding life to come back, but we also see him praying and communicating with God. Sometimes people ask, *should we pray and ask God to raise the dead, or should we use our authority and command the dead to rise?*

I would say both.

Often, when we pray, we are also hearing and communing with God so that we can position our heart, soul and mind to be in a place of faith.

Sometimes when a family member has died and there is lots of emotion, it is easy for our soul not to be in a place of faith. In the Bible we see Elisha and Peter would close the door on the family to be alone with the dead. I believe this was so they could commune with God properly, block out distractions, and step into a place of faith. It's not always possible to create this environment, but if you have the chance, I would recommend it. But ultimately, we need to live ready and be ready to raise the dead no matter what circumstances we face.

Living In Faith And Using Our Authority

We see the Biblical example of Peter praying and using his authority and that should be the same for us. We seek God in prayer, and then we use our authority!

It's all about doing life with God, co-labouring with Him and seeking His help. Then, once we're in a place of faith and our soul is settled, we go for it! We speak to that person's spirit and call them back to their body.

Praying in tongues is also a powerful tool for building our faith (Jude 1:20). There may be times that you need to take some time in prayer before you get to the person. And if you get that opportunity to raise the dead, really go into the situation with boldness and faith. Let it come from a place of communing with God and knowing your authority and knowing what the scriptures say. Go in and call that person back to life!

Modern Day Testimonies

We have looked at the Biblical data, and now I want to look at testimonies from the modern Church. Raising the dead wasn't something only for Peter and Paul, but Jesus actually encouraged all believers to raise the dead as a lifestyle. Jesus considered raising the dead a normal part of the mission.
Matthew 10:5-8 says:

These twelve Jesus sent out and commanded them, saying: "Do not go into the way of the Gentiles, and do not enter a city of the Samaritans. But go rather to the lost sheep of the house of Israel. And as you go, preach, saying, 'The kingdom of heaven is at hand.' Heal the sick, cleanse the *lepers, **raise the dead**, cast out demons. Freely you have received, freely give.* (Emphasis added).

Preaching the Kingdom, healing the sick and casting out devils; these are all things we should be practising as part of our Christian faith, and so should be raising the dead! God has given us His power and has made us brand-new creations. We are supposed to bring life to people, and one of the ways to do that is to literally raise the dead when we have the opportunity.

Many people that I know personally have seen multiple people raised from the dead. And of course, there are the past heroes of the faith such as Smith Wigglesworth and John G. Lake who had many documented cases of the dead being raised.

A friend of mine, David Hogan, has seen over sixty people raised from the dead in the last twenty-plus years of his ministry. Including his grandson!

David's grandson was bitten by a swarm of killer bees in Mexico. It's interesting because David didn't get a chance to be there in person and lay hands on the boy. Instead, he was able to pray over FaceTime, and he literally watched the spirit go back into his grandson as he was raised back to life.

I also know two people from our community who were at a David Hogan conference and heard his testimonies of raising the dead. These two people are both nurses and they were inspired by David's testimonies. So when the opportunity came for them to see two people raised from the dead, they jumped at it. They prayed the prayer of faith, and Jesus raised the two back to life!

My mentor and contributor to this book, Frank Clancy, has seen multiple people raised from the dead. I've included below one of his amazing dead raising testimonies. This will encourage you that raising the dead is absolutely still happening and that God's power is still for today!

Frank Clancy — Raising The Dead Outside Of McDonald's

Years ago now, it was about ten'o'clock in the morning when I was on my way to Church. And there was some car accident ahead of me. It turned out, a man had been drinking and got into a big fight with his wife outside of the McDonalds. The man then ran across the road, and a truck hit him.

He was on the side of the road, and all that stuff that surrounds your brain was leaking out of his head along with blood. It looked bad; it looked really bad!

I headed over to where an ambulance had turned up. I said, "Can I help mate? Can I pray for him?"

The ambulance officer said, "No! Get out of our way. We're working here. But if you really want to do something, get his wife."

You see, the man's wife was standing off to the side of the road, going off her face, yelling and cursing God.

The Ambulance officer asked me, "Can you handle her?"

So, I walked over to her and tried to get her to settle down; and she kicked me fair in the nuts! I thought, "gee, that's no good!" But I tried to settle her anyway.

Then one of the big ambulances with all the extra gear pulled up, and these guys got around her husband, connecting him to all their gear. I remember holding onto the wife because she kept trying to get in their way, yelling, screaming, and cursing God.

I said to the wife, "Instead of cursing God, He can help you. I'm a minister; let's pray together."

"No, no! God's no effing good," she said, carrying on again.

I said, "We will pray if you settle down. I'll go ask them if we can pray, but you have to settle down; otherwise, they'll tell me to nick-off."

I went over to the ambulance officers, and I asked them if we could pray. And the guy says, "No, I told you to nick-off. We've lost the man; he's dead."

At that moment, the wife went off her head. I settled her down again, and I told her, "I'm going to ask them again if we can pray now. But I need you to be fair dinkum. If you pray with me now, God will raise him up. But I need you to help me."

I go over to the ambulance officer once again, and I say to him, "I want to pray for him. Now."

The ambulance officer said, "I told you, nick-off!"

I said, "Listen, mate, he's dead now. You did all you can, and he's dead. His wife wants me and her to pray for him now. I've asked you three times already and if you don't let us, then I'm going to go to the highest authority, mate. You'll be in big trouble!"

The ambulance officer said, "Well, all right then."

I told him I want to lay hands on the body, and he said, "All right, just grab his feet."

I grabbed one foot, and the wife grabbed the other. I said to her, "You have to believe with me."

And she said, "All right."

The man had been dead for about five to ten minutes at this point with the inside of his head leaked out onto the pavement. So, we had grabbed his feet, and I began to proclaim life back into the man in Jesus's name. All-a-sudden: beep beep beep! All the machines started firing up again!

"We got him back!" Cried the ambulance officer.

I said, "No, you didn't mate. God got him back. Have you ever seen that before?"

The guy said, "I've never seen that happen before in 30 odd years being on the job."

I turned to the wife, and I said, "There you go, God got him back."

Then a big helicopter came and got him and took him off to the hospital. Two days later, I was sitting in their house, and the wife says, "He's all right now, he's all good. But I'm sorry I kicked you in the nuts!"

I believe every Christian has the ability to see the dead raised! Every Christian who is Spirit-filled has that miracle-working power within them, we just need to ignite the dynamite.

The Bible says Jesus brings life abundantly, and it is the devil who comes to steal, kill, and destroy (John 10:10). We can flip it; we can flip the switch and turn things around for the glory of God.

In summary, I think it's important to know that if we want to see revival, if we're going to ignite the dynamite, then there will be times when things get wild! Igniting the dynamite won't fit into a neat, little package of '*Sunday Church*' that is predictable and runs like clockwork. Don't get me wrong, schedules can be a good thing, but we need to be open to the move of the Spirit. Revival is messy, dynamite is explosive! Whether it's someone falling out of a window so we're now raising the dead in the middle of a Church meeting; or getting booted in the nuts because we have faith in the midst of a car accident! To ignite the dynamite, we need to be willing and ready for the fact that anything can happen.

FRANK'S JOURNEY

Before you hear about the life of Frank Clancy, I first want to state how thankful I am to God for him. Not only was he instrumental to my salvation and deliverance, but even to this day he has continued to be a major influence and mentor in my life. I thought it would be fitting to ask him to contribute two chapters to this book. I am sure you will be greatly blessed by his story and his teaching, just like I have been.

Frank Clancy

God has been really good to me, He's a very patient God!

I was brought up as a religious person where I would say the rosary every night with Mum and Dad. But I didn't know God, I didn't know Him at all. I was from a small town called Kilmore, in country Victoria. I was a wild twenty-year-old when I was selected by ballot for National Service. Out of all my friends, I was the only one drafted into the army. A lot of the other guys at the time were conscientious objectors, but I thought, maybe the army would straighten me up a bit.

As I served overseas, a lot of bad things happened, and I would drink every night. I wasn't a habitual drinker before the army, just a social drinker at parties. I didn't have an addiction until I went to Vietnam.

I remember, every time we'd go out into the bush to fight the opposing troops, I would think: *God, if you get me out of this, when I go back to camp, I promise I'll go straight to Church.* I did that a few times, and every time I got back to camp, I would just get drunk again.

I was in Vietnam for one year and one month. I had several close calls with death, and I saw good men die. I was very scared, very angry, and I would cry a lot. I grew to hate people. I came back home to Australia a very angry man and I was in a bad place.

To top things off, once I was back in Australia, I was told that two blokes from the Defence Service Homes were on their way to discuss taking my house off me because of my outstanding debt. This made me so furious, I had just risked my life serving this country in Vietnam, and now they wanted to take my house. I became so mad that I planned to grab my gun and blow their kneecaps off as soon as they approached the house. I remember thinking, *I don't care if I go to gaol.* I wasn't going to kill them, but I wanted to seriously hurt them. Now that I look back, I'm glad I didn't follow through with these dark thoughts.

The only thing that was going right during this time was that I met my wife, Denny. We were married for about a year when she fell pregnant. She struggled right through her pregnancy, and two and a half months before her due date she was taken to hospital. The doctor pulled me aside and he said, "Look, we're going to operate on Denny. You could lose her and the baby tonight."

I went down to the Catholic Church and lit all these candles. I said to God, "I know when I was in trouble in Vietnam, I called out to you and you saved me, but then I ignored you. *This time*, I promise, if you save my wife and my baby I'm going to serve you."

The next day, my daughter, Meagan, was born two and half months premature. I could hold her in the palm of my hand, and I was so excited. On the Sunday, I went to the Catholic Church, and in the middle of mass I walked straight up to the altar and got to my knees and said, "Jesus! I'm fair dinkum,
I'm going to follow you now!"

I didn't realise that this wasn't normal in the Catholic Church. A couple of the deacons tried to remove me, I shook their hands off and said, "Leave me alone, I'm talking to Jesus!"

From then on, I asked everyone about Jesus. I went to the Catholic Church, and I would read my Bible, I would read it, but I couldn't work out what was going on.

I was on a journey to find God. I knew Jesus was real, but I was scared of God-the-Father because I came from a strict, conditional relationship with my Dad. He was a beautiful Dad, but our relationship was strict.

One day I met a guy from the Assemblies of God Church, and he invited me along to his Church.

So, I said to Denny, "I'm going to this AOG Church."

Denny said, "No, we're Catholic! You can't go there!"

But I said, "I'm going, that's it. I'm going to find God."

I went to the Church, and they did an offer for salvation. They asked if anyone wanted to accept Jesus into their life. So, I went up the front and got saved and, in that moment, I understood what it was like to have a relationship with a heavenly Father.

I raced home, and I said, "Denny, guess what! I'm born again!"

She said, "You idiot, you're a Catholic!"

Denny didn't understand yet what happened, but from that day forward, I had changed. She said, "There must be a God!"

As I said before, I used to be an angry man. I would never hurt her, but I spent most of our money on alcohol and worked all the time. But after inviting Jesus into my life, I became a new man! The evidence of a true born-again experience is a changed life, and God had changed me from the inside out. Denny started to think maybe there was more to what I was saying because I had become so happy! Before then, I was so angry that people would call me *Cranky Franky!*

During this time, not only did Jesus fix up my life and character, but I also started to pray for people, and they would get healed! And not only did God honour my faith and heal through me, but amazingly, He also healed my hurts from my passed life.

You see, I still had a lot of bad memories, and anytime I saw something to do with the army, I would get angry. One morning, I was half awake, half asleep, when I had this vision. I was on the beach with Jesus and I had all these old ammunition boxes with irrigation fittings. Inside the boxes were all my horrific memories. Jesus had with Him a boat, and He asked me to hand Him the boxes to load into the boat.

I got to one box and I said to Jesus, "Not this one Jesus, I need to get this guy back." You see, I had un-forgiveness toward my old Sergeant, in fact, I hated him. He used to send us soldiers out into the heat of the battle while he would stay back in his tent at the camp. He used to always bully me and berate the troops. And I felt like I couldn't forgive him.

But Jesus said, "Hand it over." So, I gave it to Him.

We loaded the rest of the boxes into the boat, and Jesus grabbed the oars and rowed us out to the middle of the ocean. This vision felt so real that I could even hear Jesus's breathing as he rowed the boat.

Suddenly, Jesus stopped rowing the boat and He said to me, "Frank, drop them over."

I said, "No. I'm not dropping them over, Jesus."

Jesus said, "Frank, drop them over."

So, I grabbed each box and dropped them over the side of the boat. I could see the boxes drop right down to the bottom. I then came to the box that I didn't want to load into the boat. I knew the contents inside the box was about my old Sergeant who I hated.

Jesus said to me, "You need to drop that one over."

I said, "No, I'm not dropping it over. You drop it over, Jesus."

"No, you've got to do it, Frank."

"No, I'm not doing it."

And Jesus said with a tone of voice like a great mate, "Just drop it over, Frank."

I reluctantly picked up the box and dropped it over the side of the boat. I watched as it sank right down to the bottom.

Jesus said to me, "Can you see it anymore, Frank?"

I said, "No."

Jesus started rowing us back to the shore, and He said, "It's all gone now, Frank. You'll be right now." He gave me a hug, and said, "You'll be right from now on."

I woke up and everything was off me. Just like that! No therapy, no psych doctors, God just took it all away. A lot of the guys I knew in the army needed therapy. A lot of them were either killed in action, or died from suicide, or died by drug overdose because we all struggled mentally. But when I woke up, it was all gone! He pulled all the hate out of my heart, all the fear and all the depression. I felt like a million dollars, it was wonderful! One touch from Jesus can heal us in a moment. Now, I've been saved thirty-four years and I praise God for His miracle working dynamite power, it's beautiful what God can do!

DUNAMIS POWER BY FRANK CLANCY

"Bless the Lord, O my soul; And all that is within me, bless His holy name! Bless the Lord, O my soul, And forget not all His benefits: Who forgives all your iniquities, Who heals all your diseases." Psalm 103:1-3.

Praise God! You can't separate salvation and dunamis power; they go together. It goes right back to the Old Testament when King David said, *"Forget not all the Lord's benefits, who forgives all our iniquities and heals all our diseases."* Signs, wonders and miracles are a part of salvation.

The word *salvation* in the Greek is *Sozo*; which means forgiven, saved, healed, and delivered[10].

Right through the Gospels, wherever Jesus went, there was always healing and salvation together, they're never split up. When He commissioned the disciples in Luke 10 and Matthew 9, He says to them to go out and cure the people of all diseases. Not just *some diseases*, but all of their diseases! And tell them the Kingdom is at hand!

The message of the Kingdom was to be delivered with a demonstration of power. Jesus told His disciples in John 14:11-12:

Believe Me that I am in the Father and the Father in Me, or else believe Me for the sake of the works themselves. Most assuredly, I say to you, he who believes in Me, the works that I do ***he will do also; and greater works than these he will do****, because I go to My Father.* (Emphasis added).

Dynamite power is so important because Jesus told us to do miracles. He did miracles and multitudes of people came to Him. It says throughout the Gospels that multitudes came to Jesus to be healed and not just to hear His preaching. It's the same in the book of Acts, the multitudes would come to get healed, and then the disciples would preach to them!

When John the Baptist was in gaol, he sent his followers to Jesus and asked Him, *Are you the Christ or do we look for another?* Or another way to say it: *Are you the real deal? Or just another counterfeit?* Jesus said, *The blind see, the lame walk, the deaf hear, don't be offended because of this* (Luke 7:22). Jesus was saying, *I'm not a fake. These miracles confirm that I'm the real deal.* So, really, anything other than dynamite power is a counterfeit.

The Bible says that the Gospel did not come in word only but in dunamis power in the Holy Ghost and in much assurance (1 Thessalonians 1:5). Jesus didn't only preach, but His message came with miracles. Now it's our turn, and we need to deliver His message with the same demonstration of power that He did. The Bible says, *"And they went out and preached everywhere, the Lord working with them and confirming the word through the accompanying signs. Amen."* (Mark 16:20). Signs and wonders confirm the message!

The first Church understood it: Jesus told them to lay hands on the sick, and they will recover! Go cast out demons in my name, it's a command of, God! (Mark 16:15-18). There is no plan B. The disciples went out, and the Holy Ghost went with them, confirming the Word with signs and wonders! As Jesus is, so are we in this world (1 John 4:17). If you're a faithful follower of Jesus, then you should be moving in signs and wonders to validate His Word.

When Jesus sent out the disciples, He told them, *Go out there, share a meal with them, heal the sick, and tell them the Kingdom of Heaven has come near to them* (Matthew 10:5-15). Signs and wonders validate and confirm the Kingdom of Heaven.

That's one of the reasons why many in this generation don't follow God anymore. Jesus said, *If you don't believe me, believe me for the works* (John 10:38). Well, if people don't see works in the way of signs and wonders, then they won't believe. When we start doing the works of Christ the people will start believing! If Jesus needed signs and wonders and miracles to get people to come, well, we're not better than Him. We need to do the same thing! Jesus left us the example to follow Him and He gave us the command to heal the sick. It's not a variable, it's not an option. There is no plan B!

We also know that there are lots of practical ways we can help people, for example, feeding the poor and looking after them. But this should never replace the miracle working power of God. We need to display the dunamis power!

Sometimes people feel as though they don't know how to flow in signs and wonders. Faith and obedience are the same thing. If you want to work miracles, go out and lay hands on the sick! There's no formula or set way to do it. It's not what you know; it's *who* you know. If you go out there in the name of Jesus, miracles will follow.

The best way I have found is to go out and talk to people. You don't have to bring up being a Christian right away. Ask someone, *How are you? How's your family? What are you up to today?* Just have a conversation with them. Sooner or later, they will bring up something like they're sick or someone they know is sick. Then say, *Look, I believe God can heal. Can I pray for you now? Can I bless you? Let me pray for you now, and I believe God will heal you.*

Once they've agreed, just lay your hand on them, and speak to the problem. Say, *Pain go! In Jesus's name!*

You don't ask Jesus to heal the person because He's already given us the authority in His name. Always speak directly to the problem. Don't talk too much, trying to quote ten scriptures, just put your hand on them and say, *Lord bless them now, and all sickness go in Jesus's name!*

The best idea to start flowing in dunamis power is just to start stepping out, it's the only way. You could learn about driving a car, you can read the driver's book and all that stuff, but until you get out and do it you won't know, but once you do get out there, you'll realise how easy it is. There are people overseas who are illiterate but are raising the dead. There is no formula: pray in the name of Jesus and it will work! It truly is that simple.

And if someone's got a demon in them, say, *Bad spirit go! Demon go! In Jesus's name!* That's all! Jesus said, "*Behold, I give you the authority to trample on serpents and scorpions, and over all the power of the enemy, and nothing shall by any means hurt you*" (Luke 10:19). That word "*all*" literally means *all!* We have all the power over the enemy!

If I opened up my pocket and gave you all of my money that I have, well then, I haven't got any left, have I? I gave you *all* of it. In the same way, if God has given us all authority and all power, then the devil hasn't got any. We've got it all! The devil tries to convince us that we've got none, but really, we've got *all* the power. We need to be militant with the sickness. Command the disease to go, and it will go!

The first time I saw someone healed was kind of by accident. A friend of mine came around to my place, he was a bit of a drunk, and I was a bit of an old drunk, so he brought a six-pack of beer for us, and I had bought him a Bible.

I told him, "I don't feel like drinking anymore."

And He asked, "What, you can't drink anymore?"
I said, "Nah, I just don't feel like it mate."

He threw the Bible on the ground and said, "I don't want your bleeping Bible!"

Anyway, his knee had swollen up from an injury. So, I said to him, "God can fix that; I read in the Bible that if an elder would anoint the sick with oil and pray, then God would fix them up" (James 5:14-15). I thought to myself, *Well, I'm older than him! I'll pray for him!*

I went to my garage and got some two-stroke oil and I put it on his knee. I then said, "There you go, Jesus, fix that up for us." And the swollen knee went down right in front of us! I thought, *Oh gee, God heals!*

I was praying for everyone after that! I just had a simple faith. All I would pray was, "Fix that up, Lord," and God was healing people!

But then I went and told my Pastor at Church. I said, "Isn't it great, Pastor, that God heals everyone! It's fantastic!"

The Pastor said to me, "Well, God doesn't heal all the time, you know."

I thought, *Well, I've had a good run!* But then I started thinking that the next time I pray for someone, maybe God wouldn't heal them. You see, I had lost that simple faith. I lost the simplicity of just believing the Bible. It took me years to get that back because he was a Pastor, and I was a brand-new Christian, so I thought he must be correct, and I must be wrong.

I started thinking that I must have been lucky. But really, it's faith. You believe in the name of Jesus, and He will heal. The Bible says:

> *For assuredly, I say to you, whoever says to this mountain, 'Be removed and be cast into the sea,'* **and does not doubt in his heart, but believes that those things he says will be done, he will have whatever he says**. (Mark 11:23, emphasis added).

It's as simple as that. God says what He means and means what He says! When we get a bank statement telling us how much money we have in our account, we believe it enough to confidently make a withdrawal from the bank for that amount. It's the same with the Word of God; we have to take God at His Word. If it's in His Word, then it works!

I'm amazed by how many new Christians believe the Word and see the sick healed, and yet there are many older Christians that need to quote ten scriptures first because they doubt that God will heal the person.

Faith is the trigger. The Bible says, *"For indeed the gospel was preached to us as well as to them; but the word which they heard did not profit them, not being mixed with faith in those who heard it*" (Hebrews 4:2). Faith is the key to ignition! faith is the trigger to ignite the dynamite! The Bible says, "*Now faith is the substance of things hoped for, the evidence of things not seen*" (Hebrews 11:1). Faith is real; it has substance; it is the evidence of things unseen. So, when we speak in faith and believe the Word, it triggers that substance!

I work with a lot of indigenous communities, and they understand their law. When someone invokes their law, they know they have to do it. And when the indigenous read the Bible, in the same way, they know it's God's law. They say it must be true because it's God's law! They simply believe the Word. That's why in my experience, the indigenous see a lot more healing. I've had the privilege of working in indigenous communities for about 28 years. I want to tell you that what I've taught you in this chapter is not empty words. I've seen God move powerfully with thousands of salvations and healings through the dunamis power of God. And that same power is available to all believers.

So, finally I leave you with this: believe and do not doubt, and you will see the dynamite miracle working power of Jesus!

DREAMS AND VISIONS

When God pours out His Spirit, one of the supernatural phenomena we can expect are dreams and visions. The Prophet Joel foretold this when he prophesied of an end-time outpouring of the Holy Spirit. In Joel 2:28-29 it says:

> *And it shall come to pass afterward That* ***I will pour out My Spirit on all flesh****; Your sons and your daughters shall prophesy,* ***Your old men shall dream dreams, Your young men shall see visions****. And also on My menservants and on My maidservants I* ***will pour out My Spirit in those days****.* (Emphasis added).

This incredible promise of God's Spirit being poured out upon all flesh was fulfilled shortly after the resurrection of Christ. In Acts 2, the disciples of Jesus were gathered together, abiding faithfully in prayer as they waited for the promised outpouring of the Holy Spirit. Then, with the sound of a rushing wind, the Holy Spirit fell upon them and filled them all (Acts 2:1-4).

The moment after Peter received this *'power'*, he stood up in front of many and proclaimed, *"But this is what was spoken by the prophet Joel"* (Acts 2:16). Peter recognised that the dunamis, dynamite power that Jesus promised was the same outpouring foretold by the Prophet Joel! And Joel specifically pointed to dreams and visions as being a part of what was going to happen when God poured out His Spirit in the last days.

It all links together. Dreams and visions are a part of igniting the dynamite and the miracle-working power that's been poured out in Acts 2, and still continues to be poured out today!

Now, what I find very interesting is that God has always spoken to men and women throughout the Bible through dreams and visions. Particularly in the Old Testament, we see God talking to key people at key times through dreams and visions. But I believe Joel's prophecy was showing us that there's going to be an increase in these last days. It's not just for the Prophets or certain gifted people, it's for everybody! God said He will pour out His Spirit on *"all flesh"*. That's all believers! Anyone who calls upon the name of the Lord, whether male or female, young or old, sons or daughters — everyone who receives the Holy Spirit is going to have access to this beautiful gift of dreams and visions. There's a new covenant increase for all believers that is accessible for all of us today!

I want to bring some theology around this but I'm also going to share testimonies on how God has directed me in various times through dreams and visions. This has often been very significant for not only my personal life, my ministry life, but also for effective evangelism and seeing people saved. Let me start by sharing this amazing story. . .

A few years ago, I felt led by the Lord to live in a town called Noble Park, which is a part of the greater-Dandenong city in Victoria, Australia. One of the reasons I wanted to move there was because, at the time, the region was experiencing one of Australia's highest crime rates. From the moment I was saved, my heart has always been to be a light in the dark.

During this season, my desire was to learn how to ignite the miracle-working power within me. I was particularly pressing in to hear from God and spent many hours seeking Him in prayer and fasting. One night, during this time of seeking Him, I went to bed as normal and had the most incredibly vivid dream. In the dream God spoke to me and told me to get into my car and drive to Dandenong to preach the Gospel.

Immediately, I woke from the dream. It was 1am in the morning and yet I wasn't tired at all. I had so much energy it was as though I had drunk ten coffees! I was so excited because I knew God was speaking to me through the dream and that He wanted me to get into my car and drive to Dandenong. I had diligently been seeking God, desiring to hear His voice and to be used by Him. I knew this was *go* time.

I followed the direction from God's dream; I got in my car and drove straight to Dandenong. By the time I arrived, it was around 1:30am and there was no one around. It looked to be a ghost town. But I was confident that God had spoken to me in the dream. I decided to drive around the streets and seek out the opportune moment to share the Gospel.

The first people I saw, and the only people around, was a young couple at 2am sitting in the gutter drinking from a wine cask. To be honest I wasn't sure if these were the people God was meaning for me to speak to. But there was no one else around, so I thought, *They must be it*. I got out of my car and began to approach the couple.

Now, at this particular time, as I've mentioned, Dandenong and Noble Park were notorious for gang activity. There were two rival groups in particular called the Bloods and the Crips. I noticed the young man had on him a red bandana, which was the colour of the Bloods gang, and as it turned out he was one of them.

I didn't allow intimidation to shift me out of a place of faithfulness, so I began to share the Gospel with this couple as they sat in the gutter. They didn't seem to be interested in what I was sharing, but they didn't tell me to nick-off either, so I kept chatting with them. As I was sharing, I began to sense that the girl was becoming interested in what I was saying, and I began to hear God's heart for her. I said to her "Listen, I need you to know that God woke me up in the middle of the night, after giving me a dream, and told me to come here to Dandenong to tell you that Jesus loves you. To tell you that God has a plan for your life".

I went on to share the full council of God with the couple, warning them of the consequences of continuing in sin and of Hell. But I also kept emphasising to the girl that God has a plan and a purpose for her life.

After I finished talking with the young couple, I returned to my car and headed home. To be honest I felt a little disappointed. When I set out on my mission, I thought something big was going to happen. I was expecting to see maybe an angel or experience some amazing miracle or see someone saved but, in the moment, it seemed as though nothing significant had taken place.

Feeling deflated, I suddenly sensed God speaking to my heart, "*You* did what I asked you to do, well done! You were faithful and sowed the seed".

That word helped me to realign my perspective. I realised how cool it was that God had answered my prayer. I'd been desiring for Him to use me, so He gave me a dream and sent me on a midnight mission. That was pretty amazing!

The next night revealed just how amazing God's set-up truly was. I was at home in Noble Park with a friend, when we decided to walk to the local Subway to get some dinner. It was 8pm, it was dark, and we were somewhat on our guard because there had been a lot of mugging and stabbings in the area. But this didn't deter us from taking a shortcut to Subway.

Back then there was this alleyway that ran parallel with the railway line. We began to walk down the path; it was night and very dark. About halfway down this path, we noticed a girl sprawled out across the ground. I didn't immediately recognise her, but I was deeply concerned because she looked to be dead.

My friend quickly checked her vital-signs and found a weak pulse; however, she was not breathing. She was alive but unconscious and in a very bad place. My friend called for an ambulance as I began to pray. I was declaring life back into the girl's body, as well as binding the devil in Jesus's name.

Within moments of praying, life returned to the girl. She suddenly woke up, spluttering and coughing. She looked up into my face and made eye contact. And right then, that's when I recognised her. Sprawled out on the ground in front of me, having just returned from near-death, was the girl from the night before! She was the girl God had given me the dream for! She was the reason God had sent me to Dandenong in the middle of the night, to tell her that Jesus loves her and has a plan for her life!

The girl was looking at me in clear astonishment, she was freaked out, and I was freaked out! Excited, but freaked out! You can't tell me this was coincidence; we were on a dark path in a totally different town. What are the odds of us being the ones to run into her when she'd been left for dead? My friend and I had no shadow of doubt that this was God.

It turns out that the reason this young girl was in this state was because she had tried to kill herself. She had ingested a whole lot of pills, and her intention was to lay across the train tracks but she didn't make it before passing out. The reason why she wanted to end her life was because she found out that her boyfriend, the young man from the night before, had cheated on her. She had felt alone, hopeless, and rejected.

My friend and I shared the love of God with her once more and she joyfully gave her life to Jesus and later became plugged into a local Church! It's amazing that this radical encounter all started with a dream. God still speaks to people through dreams today! And the really cool thing is, it didn't just end there with this young girl.

As I mentioned earlier in the story, the young girl's ex-boyfriend was a part of the Blood's gang and the whole reason why I moved to the Noble Park area was to reach this particular gang. This girl's story was so radical that it spread like wildfire among the gang members. Her ex-boyfriend even verified for people that I really did approach them the night before she tried to kill herself saying that God had spoken to me. So, this girl was telling all her friends in the Bloods what God had done for her.

This was incredible divine timing for this testimony to be going viral, because around that same time I was actually planning an open field outreach in Noble Park. We organised a big tent, a band, and we got the word out through flyers. I personally walked up to as many gangsters as I could, inviting them to the tent meeting.

The turn-out was way more than I had expected. This girl's personal experience with God was drawing a crowd that normally wouldn't give God the time of day. Around sixty of the Bloods gang turned up at the meeting. We didn't hold back, we preached pure Biblical Gospel. We taught on the need to turn away from sin and toward righteousness and we warned of the consequence of Hell.

Some who weren't interested in the Gospel walked away, but most of them stayed. And the amazing thing was at least half of them raised their hands in response to the Gospel message!

All of this, linked back to that girl's testimony, which then links back to the dream God had given me. From that one dream, a girl's entire life was changed, and a mini revival broke out amongst one of Melbourne's most notorious youth gangs.

God still speaks to people through dreams and visions today! I believe He knew this was going to happen. He didn't cause the girl's suffering to happen, but He knew this girl's pain and He set me up to deliver to her His redeeming message.

God knew it was a two-day set-up. He knew my friend and I would want to walk to Subway, and so He set me up to be a sign and a wonder just for this girl!

Now let me unpack some of the theology around this amazing, supernatural phenomenon of dreams and visions, and let's look at some of the different types of dreams that God can release.

Warning Dreams

Warning dreams are when God intervenes to give a person a warning on a specific matter. There are times that warning dreams will address a specific sinful situation. In Genesis 20:3, Abraham had deceived king Abimelech regarding his wife. Abraham had told the king that Sarah was his sister. In thinking that she was a single woman, Abimelech sent for Sarah to make her his wife. However, God spoke to Abimelech in a dream and gave him a stern warning, saying that if he did not return Sarah then he would surely die. Abimelech restored Sarah back to Abraham and a great sin was avoided. By giving Abimelech the heads up through a dream that Sarah was actually Abraham's wife, God saved them all from grievous sin.

Another example of warning dreams is when God will warn us of impending danger. In Matthew 2:13, God warned Joseph that king Herod was seeking the baby Jesus to destroy him. In the dream, God spoke to Joseph and gave him the heads up, but

He also directed Joseph on what to do from there. We will touch on directional dreams in a moment.

God also uses dreams to warn us in our personal walk with Him. In Job 33:14-18, the Bible tells us that God uses dreams and visions to deliver warnings that keep us from wrongdoing and pride. He uses dreams and visions to speak to us personally about certain areas of our life that need correcting. He prunes us so that we may grow and warns us of the pitfalls of sin.

Directional Dreams

Another way God speaks to us is through *directional dreams*. These are dreams where God gives wisdom and direction. This could be literal geographical direction, or even guidance in decisions to be made. In Matthew 2:19, God directs Joseph to move his family to Egypt. This is similar to the warning dream God had given Joseph previously, except now God was giving Him the direction to take so that he could bring Mary and Jesus to safety.

In all the organisations that I've founded, almost every major decision has been directed by God through dreams. One example of this took place a few years ago. Ben Fitzgerald and myself had a strong sense in our hearts that God wanted to do something in Australia like He had been doing in Europe through the Awakening events - seeing thousands being saved in stadiums like in the days of Billy Graham. During this time, Ben lived in Germany, and I lived in Australia, so we were in completely different time zones and sometimes I would forget that. One time I phoned him not realising that it was 3am his time. My phone call woke him up and he says to me, *"Bro I just had a dream, you just literally woke me up out of a dream"*.

Ben began to describe his dream, telling me that in the dream we were under a stadium in Melbourne, Australia. This was really interesting because the name of our ministry is *Awakening*, so for him to have been *awakened* from a dream about hosting a mass Gospel campaign in Melbourne was no coincidence but something significant. In fact, the stadium he described from the dream was actually Marvel Stadium, the very stadium we ended up hiring to have our hugely successful Gospel campaign. For us, we knew that the dream was confirmation that we were to definitely go ahead and take the chance of hiring the stadium and gathering people from all over the country for this historic event that happened back in 2018. It ended up being the biggest evangelistic event in Australia since the days of Billy Graham.

Looking back now, I'm so glad that we recognised God's voice and leading in that dream. It was that dream that gave us the faith and confidence to step out and see history made for Jesus.

Prophetic And Futuristic Dreams

Another way God speaks to us is through prophetic and futuristic dreams. These dreams are often God revealing to us something that's going to unfold in the future.

In Daniel 7, God gave Daniel dreams and visions that were apocalyptic in nature. What this means is, the dreams were communicating to Daniel things that were going to take place in the end times concerning when God will usher in His final Kingdom.

I believe Daniel wrote these dreams down not fully understanding what he was seeing, but the modern-day Church is witnessing the dream play out and are continually interpreting it accordingly today.

Indirect Dreams

There are times that God may choose to speak to us indirectly through other people's dreams. In these cases, we need to be open to seeing what God's doing with the people around us because He may use someone to bring us a word via their dream or vision.

In Judges 7:13-15, Gideon overheard a man speaking of his dream and then his companion giving the interpretation. One man had the dream and the other was given the gift of interpretation to highlight the message from the Lord. Gideon was humble enough to listen to the interpretation of the dream and as a result Gideon trusted the Lord and was given strategy on how to defeat Israel's enemies.

I think that's a beautiful thing because we're a body. God will often use different people to speak to us because He wants us to have fellowship with one another and because He wants us to realise we need each other. The Bible says we are living stones, and we are supposed to be fitly framed together as the Church (Ephesians 2:21).

Interpreting Dreams Is A Gift

The ability to dream is a gift from God and so too is interpreting its meaning and message. As believers, we should be pressing in to hearing from God through dreams and visions but also learning how to interpret them.

In Genesis 41:25, God gave Joseph insight into the interpretation of Pharaoh's dream. Joseph was then equipped with the ability to provide Egypt with wisdom and strategy that prepared them for seven years of prosperity and then seven years of famine. What this means is that through the gift of dream interpretation, Joseph was able to gain political influence which shifted the course of an entire nation.

False Dreams And Visions

Not every dream or vision we have will be from God. In fact, God warns us of false dreams and visions; which is why it's so important that we're grounded and founded in the Word of God. We must ensure that what we are hearing and seeing in the dream realm aligns with the scriptures. If we're not diligently reading the Word of God, the enemy can work through that realm and even bring confusion and deception through dreams and visions. Jeremiah 23:32 says:

> *Behold, **I am against those who prophesy false dreams,** says the Lord, "and tell them, and cause My people to err by their lies and by their recklessness. Yet I did not send them or command them; therefore they shall not profit this people at all," says the Lord.* (Emphasis added).

And Zechariah 10:2 also gives us an example:

> *For the idols speak delusion; The diviners envision lies, **And tell false dreams;** They comfort in vain. Therefore the people wend their way like sheep; They are in trouble because there is no shepherd.* (Emphasis added).

Just as we test the prophetic gift (1 Thessalonians 5:20-21), so too must we always test dreams to see if they are from God. Deuteronomy 13:1-3 says:

> ***If there arises among you a prophet or a dreamer of dreams, and he gives you a sign or a wonder,*** *and the sign or the wonder comes to pass, of which he spoke to you,*

> ***saying, 'Let us go after other gods'***—*which you have not known*—'*and let us serve them,*' ***you shall not listen to the words of that prophet or that dreamer of dreams****, for the Lord your God is testing you to know whether you love the Lord your God with all your heart and with all your soul.* (Emphasis added).

What this teaches us is that sometimes dreams are from God, sometimes they're from the enemy, and sometimes they can just come from the soul realm. I've termed it before as '*pizza dreams*'. When we've watched a weird movie, for instance, or we've eaten too much pizza, and we go to sleep and just dream weird stuff. It's not from God, it's not the enemy, it's just from our soul.

Now, interestingly, scientists to this day don't know why we dream. There are of course theories, but no one actually knows the reason *why*.

Ernest Hartmann, who was a professor of psychiatry at *Tufts University School of Medicine*, says:

> *The most honest answer is that we do not yet know the function or functions of dreaming. This ignorance should*

not be surprising because despite many theories we still do not fully understand the purpose of sleep, nor do we know the functions of REM (rapid eye movement) sleep, which is when most dreaming occurs.[11]

Michael J Breus (Ph.D.) says, "*Science has made great progress in deepening our understanding of dreaming. Still, there is no answer to the question: Why do we dream?*"[12]. This is because dreams are often supernatural. According to science, the answer to why we dream is unknowable. But according to the Bible, God said, "*I'm going to pour out my spirit in the last days and they will dream dreams and have visions!*" It's all part of the miracle working power that's being poured out as we ignite the dynamite and become witnesses for Christ.

THE POWER OF THE GOSPEL

Never will we hear a message more important than the Gospel of Jesus Christ. That makes this chapter, in many ways, one of the most important in this book. Everything else we cover in this book about igniting the dynamite exists mostly to support the Gospel. Healing the sick, raising the dead, signs and wonders, and dunamis miracle-working power; God uses all of these wonderful supernatural works to confirm the good news of Jesus.

Now, the message in itself is powerful. Salvation through the preaching of the Gospel is the greatest miracle of all! When someone hears the Gospel, repents and believes, they become a brand-new person. They become born-again spiritually. The Bible says, *"Therefore, if anyone is in Christ, he is a new creation; old things have passed away; behold, all things have become new"* (2 corinthians 5:17).

The Gospel contains the full power of God. The Bible says, *"For I am not ashamed of the gospel of Christ, for it is the power of God to salvation for everyone who believes, for the Jew first and also for the Greek"* (Romans 1:16). That word *power*, is the same word dunamis[13] from Acts 1:8. The dunamis, dynamite power of God is in the message of the Gospel. And when it's preached, and the hearer believes, it ignites!

We see Paul conveying the same point in different words in 1 Corinthians 1:18, *"For the message of the cross is foolishness to those who are perishing, but to us who are being saved it is the power of God."* It is impossible to seperate the message of the Gospel from the power of God! I want to take some time now to unpack what this explosive message is all about.

Good News, Bad News

We know that there is no greater news than the Gospel. However, it's important to understand that there is bad news for those who do not receive the Gospel.

In Australia, we are blessed with many beautiful beaches, but our shores can also hold many dangers. To keep the people safe, these beaches are manned by Lifeguards. Men and Women who watch for danger that the public often cannot perceive for themselves.

The Lifeguard sits on his tower and diligently watches, forever searching for an opportunity to pull someone from the bad news of unperceived danger. When the Lifeguard sees the person in need, he rides out on his jet-ski and tosses them the lifesaver. Sometimes the person cannot immediately perceive the danger they are in, such as a shark lurking beneath or a potentially deadly rip. But when they place their trust in the Lifeguard and grab hold of the lifesaver, they are pulled to safety.

Likewise, there are people drowning in sin who sometimes do not perceive the danger they're in. They may believe their life is smooth waters, yet they are blinded to the current of sin, and the demons which lurk below, waiting to drag them down to the depths of hell. They do not realise the bad news, which is, unless they place their trust in the lifesaver, they will perish.

The Gospel is the lifesaver. And it's important that people understand the bad news before they can see the necessity of the good news of the Gospel, and why it's the power of God unto salvation.

Who We Were

> Ephesians 2:3-5 says,
> *Among whom also **we all once conducted ourselves in the lusts of our flesh, fulfilling the desires of the flesh and of the mind, and were by nature children of wrath,** just as*

the others. But God, who is rich in mercy, because of His great love with which He loved us, even when we were dead in trespasses, made us alive together with Christ (by grace you have been saved). (Emphasis added).

Paul's language in this passage is amazing, he uses words such as, *"once," "were,"* and *"have been."* So, immediately we know that Paul is referring to the past-tense. Our nature before being saved was a wretched one. This passage reveals that humanity is born into a sinful nature and is in need of redeeming. When writing to the Roman Church, Paul said, *"for all have sinned and fall short of the glory of God"* (Romans 3:23). We are all sinful by nature from birth.

Not only is humanity born as children of wrath, but in the same passage Paul states that we were *dead in our trespasses* (Ephesians 2:5). This is referring to a spiritual death. Another way to describe it is to say that people who aren't born-again are infected with the *disease* of sin.

However, Paul then says, *"But God, who is rich in mercy, because of His great love with which He loved us, even when we were dead in trespasses, made us alive together with Christ (by grace you have been saved)"* (Ephesians 2:4-5). Paul first gave the bad news but then immediately he brings the good news! It is so important when preaching the Gospel that we explain to people the bad news so that they can receive the good news.

The whole world has been infected with something that is far greater than any disease known to mankind, whether it be black plague, HIV, cancer or COVID-19. It is the spiritual disease of sin that not only affects us in this life but also the one to come!

The crazy thing about this disease is that many are living their lives without knowing that they are infected. They could be walking and talking and experiencing feelings, going through the emotions of life, without actually knowing that they are spiritually dead in their transgressions and are disconnected from God. This is why it's imperative to preach the truth! We need to warn people about their spiritually dead state. They don't need to stay dead in their trespasses; Jesus can make them alive!

Another example of what is the bad news and the good news is found in Romans 5:10. Here we see the Bible also says that we were once enemies of God. *"For if **when we were enemies** we were reconciled to God through the death of His Son, much more, having been reconciled, we shall be saved by His life"* (emphasis added). The good news of reconciliation and eternal life is in this verse, but so is the bad news. Before we were in Christ, we were enemies of God. People need to recognise their need for a Saviour because the devil blinds people from realising that they are enemies of God (2 Corinthians 4:4). Jesus said, *"He who is not with Me is against Me, and he who does not gather with Me scatters abroad"* (Matthew 12:30). There is no neutral ground in the Kingdom. You are either all in for Jesus, or not at all. Whether you realise it or not, the Bible says that people without Jesus are enemies of God and that's why they need the good news.

Isaiah 59:2 also reveals the bad news that we were once separated from God. It says, *"But your iniquities have **separated you from your God**; And your sins have hidden His face from you, So that He will not hear"* (emphasis added). Before we were born-again, our sin had built a wall of separation between us and God. God hates that! He wants to smash that wall down! He's not willing for any to perish (2 Peter 3:9) but He wants to be reconciled to us and have relationship with us.

Ephesians 2:14 says, *"For He Himself is our peace, who has made both one, and has broken down the middle wall of separation."* That's good news! But if we don't repent from sin and become born-again, then we don't receive His peace and we remain separate from God. Jesus died on the cross so that we could be reconciled to Him and to bring down the middle wall of separation.

We were once by nature children of wrath, dead in our trespasses, and separated from God. But that's when the Gospel comes into play. When people understand the message of the Gospel, believe it, and make the decision to repent, that's when the miracle-working power, the dynamite, ignites and destroys the work of the devil. The disease of sin is destroyed, chains are broken, and they become a brand-new person. But first, they must understand the importance of repentance. Let me share with you a story about my sister, Sarah.

My Sister, Sarah.

There was a time when my sister, Sarah, thought she was right with God, but in reality, she wasn't fully walking with Him. Sarah thought she was saved, and she would profess to know Jesus, but her life wasn't bearing the fruit of repentance (Matthew 3:8).

Sarah was an alcoholic, she wasn't plugged into Church life, and she wasn't abiding in prayer or reading her Bible. In reality

Sarah wasn't really interested in Christianity. Yet if you asked her about her beliefs, she would still profess to be a Christian because it was her up-bringing.

A few years after I encountered God and became born again, I sensed that I needed to challenge my sister to turn from sin and fully embrace Jesus. I knew chances were, Sarah wouldn't like me confronting her with the truth, and that potentially our brother-sister relationship would be put on the line, but I also knew that her eternal soul mattered way more than what she thought of me in that moment.

I met with Sarah and opened my Bible to James 2:19, telling her, *"You believe that there is one God. You do well. Even the demons believe—and tremble!"*.

I told my sister, "You can say you believe, but that doesn't make you a Christian. A superficial belief won't get you to Heaven. Even the devil believes, and trembles!"

Sarah became so mad with me! It's interesting that you can tell someone "Jesus loves you" and they probably won't get mad at you. They may even respond, "Thanks, He loves you too". But the problem is, if you leave it at just that sometimes people can think they're good with God when they're not. They can go on with their lives thinking they're going to Heaven when really, they're on their way to hell!

Don't get me wrong, sometimes when we talk to people, we may only have time to say, "Jesus loves you". And a seed is better than nothing! We've seen some amazing encounters and outcomes from people by simply telling them that Jesus loves them. But, if we only ever leave it at that, then people will be like devils who haven't been converted in their hearts. Sometimes speaking the hard truth brings persecution, but we must not be ashamed of the Gospel.

With all that in mind I shared with my sister the hard truth and she did become angry with me. She was so mad that I had to leave her house! Sarah wanted to hear nothing more from me.

As I left her house, I remember wondering if I had done the right thing. In the natural, Sarah's immediate reaction seemed to push her further away from me, and my concern was that I had pushed her further away from God.

However, I later found out something powerful happened after I left her with that scripture!

You see, the Bible says that the Word of God is like a two-edged sword (Hebrews 4:12) and it cuts through to the very core of our being. And Jesus said, "*And you shall know the truth, and the truth shall make you free*" (John 8:32).

Once I left Sarah's house, the Holy Spirit had begun to work on her. Later she told me that what I shared with her convicted her so deeply that she ended up on her knees on the kitchen floor with tears streaming down her face as she repented!

Sarah told God, "Jesus, I'm sorry, I give you my whole life!".

The Bible says the Holy Spirit comes to convict the world of sin, righteousness and the judgement to come (John 16:8). If the Holy Spirit is convicting the world of sin, righteousness and judgement to come, then it's important that the message we preach aligns with Him! We don't want to be working against the Holy Spirit, telling people that they're okay in their sin when really the Holy Spirit is trying to bring them life-saving conviction!

The Gospel is powerful when it's preached in its entirety and fullness. When we preach the Gospel in truth, it has the power to transform lives and create true born-again believers.

Repent And Believe

When preaching the Gospel, we must communicate that salvation is a free gift in Jesus. Paul said, *"by grace you have been saved"* (Ephesians 2:5). People only need to believe and receive it by faith. Then they must repent. The message of repentance is vital when preaching the Gospel. Repentance means to do a complete U-turn. We must tell people that they need to make the decision to turn away from sin, to turn away from the very disease that kills them spiritually. They must choose to come out of darkness, change the way they think, and decide to no longer sin.

After turning from sin the next part of repentance is to turn to God. They turn to His ways and His Word and they choose to walk the narrow path. The path may be hard, but it's the path that leads to eternal life! When people make this decision it's the empowering force of grace that changes them from the inside out and enables them to live out this new life of Christianity.

Everyone Needs The Saviour

When discipling new believers, or potential new believers as we've stated previously, it's important that they understand why it is they need the Gospel. The Gospel is not just the power of God unto salvation for a select few, the Gospel is for all people! It's not only for bad people, or hurting people, or for those that need some sort of religious crutch to help them through life. Every single person is in need of the Saviour. Every person needs the Good News!

I will often strike up conversations with strangers and share with them my testimony about salvation. One of the common responses I hear is, "Oh I'm glad it's worked for you." In other words, they're saying, "I've got my thing that I do for my life and I'm glad religion worked for you, but it's not for me". Here's the thing; it doesn't matter how good they think they are, or even how good society thinks they are, or how great a sportsman they are, or a musician, or even how wonderful a family person they are. The truth is every single human-being has been infected with sin. The main aim of the Gospel is not to necessarily make someone's life better but rather to see people reconciled back to God and in relationship with Him. And God is not willing that anyone would perish and suffer eternal torment (2 Peter 3:9). The Gospel is not just a good idea; it's the only cure that every human being needs.

This is really important, and I would encourage believers to use certain key verses to explain this when sharing the Gospel. One such verse is Romans 3:23, *"for all have sinned and fall short of the glory of God."* This scripture presents the bad news that we have all fallen short in our sin. But then we can also share with them Romans 6:23, which says, *"For the wages of sin is death, but the gift of God is eternal life in Christ Jesus our Lord."* Combining those scriptures, in short, sums up the most important parts of the Gospel. The bad news is first stated and then the good news is presented. Everyone has sinned and everyone must understand that the penalty for sin is spiritual death. But the good news is that the gift of God is eternal life through Christ Jesus our Lord! That is where the power is if they would receive the message and believe. John 3:16 says, *"For God so loved the world that He gave His only begotten Son, that whoever believes in Him should not perish but have everlasting life."* Believing activates the power that makes you a brand-new person! When we believe, God literally breathes new life into us!

The Good News

When we accept the free gift of salvation and repent by turning away from our sin and toward God, we literally become brand-new! 2 Corinthians 5:17 says, *"Therefore, if anyone is in Christ, he is a new creation; old things have passed away; behold, all things have become new."* Christianity is not a self-help fad. The message of the cross is revolutionary! When we enter into relationship with Jesus, our entire lives are transformed. Our culture changes; it's no longer the world's culture, or Australian culture, or any other culture; we become a part of Kingdom Culture. We become brand-new from the inside out. Our spirit is no longer diseased with sin. We no longer have condemnation hanging over our shoulder. The wages of sin have been paid by Christ, and we have become justified through faith. We no longer have a sinful nature.

The Bible says in 2 Peter 1:4, *"by which have been given to us exceedingly great and precious promises, that through these you may be partakers of the divine nature, having escaped the corruption that is in the world through lust"*. Previously we unpacked how, by nature we were children of wrath. But the good news is that the power of God has transformed us into partakers of His divine nature! Our old nature no longer exists; Jesus has given us His righteousness, and we have become holy through the power of the Holy Spirit. And now, as disciples, we learn to walk this out. The Bible says Romans 3:23-26,

> *for all have sinned and fall short of the glory of God, being **justified freely by His grace** through the redemption that is in Christ Jesus, whom God set forth as a propitiation by His blood, through faith, to demonstrate His righteousness, because in His forbearance God had passed over the sins that were previously committed, to demonstrate at the present time His righteousness, that He might be just and the justifier of the one who has faith in Jesus.* (Emphasis added).

That word *justified* (v23), means declared or made righteous in the sight of God. The good news is, born-again believers have been made righteous in the sight of God, and we are also reconciled back to God!

Previously we unpacked how we were His enemies, but the good news is that once born-again, not only do we become His friends we also become part of His family! We are sons and daughters of God! This is why the Gospel is so powerful; the Gospel takes a sinner, an enemy of God and makes that person a beloved Child of God. 1 John 3:1 says, *"Behold what manner of love the Father has bestowed on us, that we should be called* **children of God!** *Therefore, the world does not know us, because it did not know Him."* God, in His great love, is now described as our Father. We are now sons and daughters of a great heavenly Father who loves us very much and it all happened by faith and grace! That's who we now are in Christ Jesus! That's the miracle of the Gospel! That's why the Gospel is such good news!

In summary, not only is the dynamite power of God used to see phenomenal signs and wonders such as the sick healed and the dead raised; but it's also important to understand the Gospel itself contains this dynamite power. When we preach the full Gospel it has the potential to ignite the greatest miracle of all: salvation!

REFERENCES

1 Strong's Concordance: G5331

2 Strong's Concordance: G1411

3 https://brisbanehealingrooms.com/who-is-john-g-lake/

4 Strong's Concordance: G907

5 Strong's Concordance: G5331

6 Strong's Concordance: H4540, Oxford Languages

7 Strong's Concordance G4991

8 Strong's Concordance: H7495

9 https://twitter.com/drmichaellbrown/status/1231622108708515843

10 Strong's Concordance: G4982

11 https://www.scientificamerican.com/article/why-do-wedream/

12 https://www.psychologytoday.com/au/blog/sleep-newzzz/201502/why-do-we-dream

13 Strong's Concordance: G1411

www.ingramcontent.com/pod-product-compliance
Lightning Source LLC
Chambersburg PA
CBHW070254010526
44107CB00056B/2459